DI

IN THE STILLNESS,

DIANA

IN THE STILLNESS, EVERYTHING HAPPENS

A BOOK BY DIANA NOT ABOUT DIANA

ANNE STEWART

CONTENTS

ACKNOWLEDGEMENTS

There are too many people to mention because, as in both our cases, and in everyone else's, every person we have met for good or ill has brought us to this place.

So, it is easier, quicker and most appropriate merely to acknowledge the amazing eternal Spirit that manifested as Diana Spencer, known to millions as Princess Diana from 1961 to 1997.

However, there is one honourable exception. Joe Fox.

Joe would go out of his way to help anyone. He had an amazing dry wit, cared deeply about animals and was the partner of a very dear friend of ours, Sue Wrench. He passed away suddenly and unexpectedly in the summer of 2010.

INTRODUCTION

*'You have been chosen, and you chose
to be on this planet now.'*

If you were to describe the current state of the world to a visitor from another planet, would that description include the words, Love, truth, compassion, tolerance, justice, peace, abundance, beauty, equality and connectedness?

No?

But surely that is the kind of world we all want.

So what is stopping us?

In removing the obstacles to a healed planet, an Earth free from war, famine, disease, corruption, manipulation, greed, contempt, ignorance, exploitation and control, might we need some help?

HELP IS AT HAND

We have been blessed over millennia with giants of Love, wisdom and compassion. These people were role models of the last century we looked to for loving acts, for forgiveness, for selflessness, and for guidance?

Diana Spencer's wedding in 1981 attracted a TV and radio audience of 1 billion. During her adult life she was consistently rated the world's most famous woman. Her 1997 funeral was viewed by half the planet's then population (2.5 billion). One of the reasons Diana attracted such world-wide attention is her appeal as 'Queen of Hearts'. Her compassion, her Love of humanity and those 'less fortunate' than herself shone out, as even her most hardened critics would have to admit. Here is how she put it:

'Nothing brings me more happiness than trying to help the most vulnerable people in society. It is a goal and an essential part of my life - a kind of destiny. Whoever is in distress can call on me. I will come running wherever they are.'

Now, if you believed that the soul that was known as Diana Spencer gave up her 'destiny' as soon as she left the 'Earth plane', you would be very much mistaken. In the world of Spirit, she has become a focal point for the efforts of all those who wish to work with humanity and release the world from its current prison.

Anne Stewart was never particularly interested in Diana, and I (Jack) have always had republican (anti-hereditary privilege) leanings. But Anne 'answered the call' one night in June 2011, when Diana appeared in her bedroom. Having overcome the shock, Anne agreed to work with Diana to help transform the world. So how can someone in Spirit, however famous and inspirational when 'here', working with a relatively unknown person as their 'voice' have such an impact?

We only need a fraction of the billions who felt a connection to Diana to turn to her again in Spirit. The only way to change this world is through LOVE. Connecting to 'source energy' or God if you prefer. Loving and accepting ourselves, loving others, forgiving the abusers and the abused. And, as Love infuses enough people on the planet, as the fault lines of division fall away, as the light of God shines in the darkest corners, all that will eventually remain of those who are currently directing the chaos will be a memory.

This book can change your life. It will bring to your attention revelations about how things really are. You will discover how to counter the fear agenda. You will let go of DOUBT.

You will discover how to revert to living as the heart-centred being you first were, realising that the combination of the ego and intellect has taken us to the very edge of the precipice, within a whisker of 'Armageddon'.[1]

You will learn how to let go of your own physical and mental pain. You will learn how to heal others. You will learn how to contribute to healing the planet, the whole of humanity and all sentient beings.

And you will learn how the world is heading now towards paradise, re-claiming our birth right and birth place.

If you are open to this possibility, as you read these words they will resonate with you. Because *we all must participate in this process*. It can no longer be left to others who have abused our trust. We can longer give our power away.

As you read this book you will realise that you are 'powerful beyond measure.'

Diana's wish, and that of the world of Spirit, is to 'take the planet to another dimension'. To do this we must first awake, heal ourselves and each other, and then come together in knowing that Love is the greatest power in the Universe.

You may not yet believe all this is very simple but then you haven't read the book. And, if it still matters, you will find out why and how Diana chose Anne...

Introduction

FOREWORD

BY MARK W FOSTER

I'll keep this short and simple, the book you hold in your hands right now is a gift borne out of pure Love and to read it is to immerse yourself in that immense Love.

Every page exudes the deep compassion and feelings of genuine Love that a parent has for a new-born child. Love expressing from beyond the physical veil and Love expressing in this physical experience meet to create this gift for humanity. I do not use these words lightly because as Anne and Jack know I did not read this book quickly I felt my way through every wondrous page and then reread it several times as the content is so good.

As Diana explains in the book the mind or more accurately the left brain, has been over stimulated and effectively hijacked. This leads us to go on an endless search for information, we read a book and think we know the core ideas in it and on some level, we do.

However we only know it on an intellectual level, we have an awareness of what the book told us, yet unless we take the time to absorb and feel the power of the words in it and then apply them in our lives, then we have missed an golden opportunity for growth.

I would be doing you and the book a great disservice if I did not point out that this is never more important that with the very book you hold right now. You literally have the keys to kingdom placed in your hands, yet for some they will throw them away, they will read or even scan read it, say 'yes I know it now, what a lovely book' and move on, storing the information in their already cluttered minds, how truly sad.

Whether you choose to believe it or not you have caused this powerful material to be in your life for a reason, it is an attempt by a part of you that loves you deeply to provide what you need to help you get through these challenging times we are all facing.

Please do not miss the golden prize you have now found and go on searching for the answer. You asked for it, you attracted it, you have it now and this is the real deal.

I have experienced Diana's energy and actually seen her morph over Anne in a workshop, the Love coming through that wonderful being is so powerful, so emotional and yet so graceful. You will feel it too if you take the time to be with the book, go beyond the words and feel the Love behind them and that put them there.

This gift of true Love is without doubt a timely antidote for our troubled times, a route map to guide us back onto our Divine path. Unlike some spiritual books it does not seek to avoid, duck or sidestep the dark side of events on the planet currently, instead choosing to bring awareness and loving light to those situations, and by sharing with us powerful practical energetic tools, guides us to heal and transform ourselves and the world.

Enjoy and savour this gift, it is not a huge book for a reason, for like gold, quality does not need to come in great quantities to be of immense value. In fact, if this book was made of solid gold it could not be more valuable to you than it is right now. So let Diana take you tenderly by the hand and guide you with loving help of two wonderful souls Anne and Jack, on a journey of profound remembering, healing and soul discovery, unlike any other.

Mark W Foster, Energy Coach & Author

THE BEGINNING,

ANNE'S FIRST CONTACT WITH DIANA

Anne Stewart's biggest trauma was the completely unexpected and tragic death of her mother with a brain haemorrhage in 1981. As she was recovering from the grief and loss of her best friend as well as the person who had brought her into the world, Anne realised her own psychic and healing abilities had been awakened.

(Spiritual) healing is the path she chose, and she has helped hundreds of people over the last 30 years. More recently, she has also attended workshops to allow her to develop as a psychic and medium.

One such workshop, held in Stockport, nr. Manchester, England in summer 2010 was conducted by, amongst others, famous UK mediums Mavis Pitilla and Tony Stockwell. At that workshop, which was attended by around 100 people, Anne was given this 'channelled' message by a complete stranger:

I come to you with Love and only Love.
It is what we are.
It is all that there is and ever will be.
Embrace that thought and embrace it now.
It is all that you will ever need to know.
Trust. Trust in us as we trust in you. We are with you always, one and the same.
You are never alone and in your sorrow we sit with you.
The path is golden and straight – simply carry yourself forward and when you are tired we will carry you.
'Til we meet again my friend, 'til we meet again.
Shalom.'

At the time, she had no idea what this was about, despite it resonating very deeply with her.

Over six months later, early in 2011, several psychic friends of hers predicted, in varying degrees of detail, that when we moved into our new house (in Grappenhall, south Warrington, Cheshire, UK) she would be 'helped' by a new Spirit guide. The name Saint Agnes was mentioned.

One night in June she recalls feeling a pull on her shoulder. She awoke and 'saw' (as real as a living person) Diana at the side of the bed.

(About one week before, she had a couple of vague dreams about Diana playing with her two sons. She dismissed them of no significance).

Shocked, she remembers recovering enough to mumble 'What do you want?' The reply was 'I want to work with you through the heart. I've been watching you for some years. There is so much work we have to do, and we have little time left.' Anne was still dazed when she agreed, and soon after Diana faded from sight.

For the next few days, Anne kept this experience to herself, not knowing how 'real' it was, feeling very emotional and doubting her sanity.

Speaking to her psychic friends again, in an attempt to get back to 'normality', they concurred it was real, and she should be honoured and welcome this revelation. Slowly, hesitatingly, she did. One night 'the channelling' occurred in my presence and we recorded it on a dictaphone. The essence of the message was that Diana's death was pre-destined and it was the way to open hearts that could not be opened in any other way.

Anne's first public performance was on our 'Healing the Spirit' show on MBS Lifestyles live internet TV on 25/8/11. Since then she has continued to receive guidance from Diana. A few more 'live' channellings ensued, but it wasn't until January 2012 that the real 'work' began.

In the early hours of three mornings, the 25th, 26th and 27th of January, Anne was woken up and retired to the room next door to write down the second chapter of the book. As you will discover, these short sessions introduce many of the main themes covered in subsequent chapters. That is the delicate state of the planet, taking responsibility for changing it (and not blaming God), dropping into the heart, taking control of our thoughts, the collapse of the 'old order', (re) aligning ourselves with God, and how to be aware of and remove the toxicity from our diet.

The remaining chapters contain sixteen formal channellings, which were recorded and faithfully (I trust) written up over a period from March to July 2012. The very last entry was channelled in July 2013. The notes which accompany each chapter can be found at the back of the book. These notes are exclusively (except where Diana is re-quoted) mine. After the notes, we have 'Tools and Techniques', a list of all the things Diana has suggested you can do on a regular and occasional basis to turn your life around. The appendices contain explanations of chakras (A), and breathing techniques (B). Further information is given about Anne and myself at the very end of the book as are details of Diana Divine Healing workshops and Diana Energy Healing products.

Only two books have been used as direct reference material, and their details are given in the notes section.

And St. Agnes? The earliest reference is to an Agnes who lived in Rome from 291 to 304. The small village of St. Agnes in Cornwall is another connection. Diana told Anne that St. Agnes was one of her earlier incarnations...

A book *by* Diana, not *about* Diana...

Jack Stewart

In beautiful Malvern, Worcestershire UK,
enjoying a real summer in July 2013.
Last 'summer' it never stopped raining,
but as Diana said, 'it was cleansing the Earth'.

JANUARY 25-27TH 2012

25/1/2012

[For this and the next 16 chapters, Diana's words are written in regular font style. When Jack asks a question, it is always in italics. Where Anne herself comments, it is in italics too.]

Welcome my friends. I am so pleased once more to be with you, and to be able to communicate with you. It saddens me to see your world as it is at present, so much has gone on for aeons, the Earth is at breaking point and Mother Earth weeps with sadness.

We have taken advantage of her for so long and it has to stop; our/your Earth is so beautiful, and God has given you so much, enough for every need to be met but there are the greedy amongst you and the selfish.

We have to consider future generations and the children, we have to take control of all our thoughts and actions; it is no use blaming God for all the wrong doings. It is us. We have choice and responsibilities; we don't have to live in conflict either with ourselves or others. Look within your own heart, be guided by your heart, listen to your heart, do not be misguided by the ego; the mind has for so long been fed a tissue of lies and it does not know the truth any more. We can and must tame the mind.

By changing our thoughts we can change our energy, energy within the body, to make the body stronger and healthier. It is our duty to educate and nurture others. Health is our birthright, being unhealthy and ill is not our natural state.

We now have great opportunities to resolve our health and thought patterns.

The world is on the brink of changing; old ways are going and are being brought to the forefront to be cleansed. We all have our part to play; it is no use blaming each other. Whilst the Earth is broken and polluted it can all be changed. Each and every one of you has a duty, for it cannot proceed the way it has.

Dark, negative energies and forces are coming to the forefront like never before. Look around and whilst everything appears chaotic, I can assure you it is very timely and ordered; we are on the brink of new beginnings though it might appear frightening and scary. Changes will be so much for the better; the world has a chance of going forward in Love and light.

Focus your thoughts on the beauty of it all, create your own world. Whilst there is still much work to be done, the light energies have been working towards this time for many years. Take heart and know that you are protected with the light.

You are a human being, living in a speck of time here on Earth, but your presence is known to the higher ones and you have been chosen, and you chose to be on this planet now. While you may not know the higher beings have been working with your planet you may lighten as the energies of the planet are changing and clearing. We can now get closer to you as your vibration gets lighter, we can work with and through you. You have much work to do.

You have the seasons of life on your planet all orchestrated by God to give you life and to sustain you. The cycle of life, your life, your very life is so precious. If only you knew how precious it was to all us here in the higher realms. We are here to help you to be with you and to Love you.

Until we meet again. Let the tears of the planet turn to joy.

26/1/2012

Good evening, or should I say morning. Each and every one of you is loved by God. If only you would realise that, how different your life would be.

Everything is provided for you; we in the higher realms watch you struggle and it makes our hearts heavy. If you ask and believe your life could be so joyous and carefree. God only wants the best for all his children. You have become so separated from your Father in Heaven, but all is not lost. Align yourself with God.

When you are aligned you have your power – you all as individuals are so powerful – reconnect with your source and you will see your life will change. You all have been so disconnected in your world. Pray to God, pray for each other. The power of prayer is indescribable.

Lift up your hearts and become one with God and each other and feel your magnificence. Go deep into your heart and feel the Love and joy.

You look outside of yourself for these things, in material things, but you will find no long-standing joy or peace there. It may give you pleasure for a brief time.

27/1/2012

Good morning. I want to talk to you about your food and diet. At this time, with the planetary changes, your diet is of extreme importance.

I watch with horror at some of the food that some of you eat. Do you not realise what it is doing to your mind and body? The red meats and burgers are toxic for your body, and especially the digestive system. If you could see how that burger, that sausage, that chicken got to your dinner table you would be appalled.

[There is] so much cruelty to your animals that we here in the higher realms watch with horror. As you digest these foods, you are putting toxins in yourselves. Imagine the fear of that animal before it is killed. That fear is communicated in the animal's cells, and you are eating that fear. And that fear adds to the fear that is rampant on your Earth.

You are eating and digesting fear. And fear is everywhere.

Help yourself, cleanse yourself; eat organic food when it is possible. Or from your local farm shops. Not food that has been flown half way around the world, where the energy of this food is destroyed.

Use vitamins; selenium, magnesium, vitamin C. These can help nourish the body and are vital for organ replenishment.

Look to each other, care for each other, care for the animal kingdom. See how many animal species you have. God has thought of everything for you to have a wonderful experience while you are here. But you do not listen to his teachings, you would rather listen to the lies told by your media and the lies that keep you in total fear. You do not have to live in fear as so many of you are living your daily lives.

This is not what God meant life to be for you. He gave you free will and choice. See beyond this 'reality', stand up for yourself and be counted. Did God not say that He knew how many hairs were on your head? God knows what you are all going through so turn your thoughts and Love to God and trust in Him to provide.

Does it not say in your 23rd psalm 'he prepared a table for me in the midst of my enemies; my cup overflows?' Your cup should be overflowing with your Love for God and Love for each other.

I will leave you with Love in my heart for each and every one of you.

Goodnight.

[Anne didn't have any further formal channelling with Diana for two months, apart from episodic 'visits.' We had a lot of Healing Code workshops all over the UK planned for this time and, interestingly, the next session came after our return from a successful series of workshops in Greece.]

CHAPTER ONE

MARCH 26TH 2012

Well it's great to be here again and it seems so long since we spoke. Things here are going much faster now and we have a lot of work to do and we have to get on with this work.

You will notice I have linked up with your healer friend Harry[2], and by doing this we are working together to accelerate the healing. Things are spinning, spinning; spinning so fast that we here in Spirit can hardly hold on. And we know what it is like for you on the Earth plane. We are all here guiding; we are all helping. You are never alone. As I said earlier when we spoke that my role and my way was to end my life as it did and, although this might have sounded strange to you, you will understand now that all these years on I need to be here in Spirit. I can use you and work with you more than with all the people on the Earth plane to get the Spirit message through. The message of Jesus. The way forward. The only way we can move forward as I've said before is caring and sharing and loving each other.

Even though my time on Earth was very painful in many areas, through many ups and downs as you will say in your world; of having Love and losing Love, having eating problems and health problems, and the pain of having to share the boys. I can use all this now I am in Spirit. I can feel all the turmoil I can feel all the hurts, and depressions and anxieties. We are moving closer and closer now to much better times, but we have to work – we can't just sit back.

We need to cleanse ourselves and cleanse the Earth. New ways are coming, new ways I will show you. We are formulating them here in Spirit. In the next few weeks and months we will have all this ready for you. We will enable people to heal themselves without the pills and without the medicines.

There is so much to say and so quickly do I need to say it. We will talk now about the cells, and I know that you and Jack work with the Healing Code[3]; I want to go into this in some great depth. The cells of our body contain so much information – information that has gone back years – hundreds and thousands of years. Some of this information is full of all kinds of emotions, hatred, Love – mixed deep emotions. Mostly negative. This is true of nearly every person on the Earth plane. So these cells do need to be cleared. And you and Jack are doing a wonderful job in doing this. We need to make it simple and we need to make it clearer to people how important this is. For without these cellular memories being cleansed and taken away the work is only half done.

The negativity has been on the land for thousands and thousands of years, and we are now coming to a new time, a golden time. And as we clear our own cells we clear the negativity of the planet. We need to educate people more. We will be working on formulas do this. It is so easy to do, yet people will not accept the simplicity of the way we can cleanse ourselves.

The cells hold vital information and, as you know and as you teach, each cell knows what the other cell is doing. It is great information. In and out, in and out goes the information. But the information needs to be positive. But we need to get rid of the deep, deep hatred, anger, lust and all the emotions that have been buried so long in our cellular memory and also in the Earth.

We can rid ourselves of illness and disease – our bodies were never meant to be like that – also cut out all pills and medication. We will get to a time on this Earth plane where the old methods being used at the moment will just disappear. And we will heal ourselves through our breath, through our eyes, and through our Love for each other.

The carving up of the body, the cutting of the body, is so unnecessary. Our bodies were never meant to be cut and to be sawed like they are today. As we do that, as surgeons cut into the body, it is having an amazing effect, [a] negative effect on the body. Shock effect. Just unbelievable. We here in Spirit know and can see what's happening when people go and have these operations. Some of these are necessary, but we know a lot are not. The Healing Code is so easily done without operations or medication. This will take time, but we are working on it here in Spirit world.

You are aware of how much water affects the body. And how water holds the information that you need.[4] It is so important, the water. The water has to be as clear and clean as possible. Also, you know about the messages and information that is gathered in the water.[5] And this is where it holds [information] within our cells. Again this needs to be cleansed out. We will tell you more about this in the next few sessions and in the next few weeks.

I have said before how important your food is. We can talk about that later. There is new information coming through that will be encoded into your codes, into every human being on the planet. These will be lighter vibrations and it may cause pain and some discomfort, as I've already said in earlier sessions. We ask that you just bear with us on this. We know it will be too painful for some, but this new coding will bring Love and light into the world. If we don't do this then we will have many thousands of years living in the way the negativity has been displayed for all these times and for all these aeons.

The planet is being saved, even though we have been and are at a tipping point, but that tipping point is slightly now going into our favour. We know we have a lot of you working, and spreading the word. It is going fast but we do need to accelerate this. People will and are becoming aware, and will take notice. People are longing now for something different from the old ways, they are really getting so fed up with the politicians and the lies, the anguish, the cheats. Everything is now coming to the surface and there will be more and more. Some of it will be painful, some of it will be laughable, and some of it will be so stupid that people will not understand how some people can behave. But they will be shown up for what they are; the media itself is starting to crack. You will find the media is starting to change, looking for more positive ways, because they know they will be losing the battle in the months and the years that are coming. They will not be able to spread this darkness that they are allowed to do at the moment. And one or two of your papers are thinking and are looking for ways to do this. And you will notice this. There is so much work being done. And we are so pleased here. And it has accelerated beyond what we had hoped for. But again, we need to keep pushing and pushing, and pushing it out. And we need like-minded people, like yourselves and lots of other people that you can inform and you [can] integrate with.

We have talked about the coming together of the Essenes.[6] This is so, so very important. The Essenes are now coming through. You will meet people from the Essenes, you will know immediately. As I know you are aware anyway. You will know immediately when you meet these people. They are special, they work from the heart only and they work for the comfort of the people and the animals and the planet. They are very much into food, and the way we store and keep our food and the chemicals. Yes, thank God, people are waking up to it all. So you see, we have many, many things here to do, and you will be amazed at some of the unseen things that are going on in your world that we are working behind the scenes on. We have hundreds of thousands of our Spirit friends here that are working towards your planet.

Take note now of the fruits. Be wary and watchful of the fruits. Fruits that are coming into the supermarkets. Check them because they are being filled with chemicals. A lot of these chemicals will affect your body. They will dumb you down, they will give you aches and pains, and they will make you listless and tired. You will not expect this from fresh bright fruit. But do be very wary and, where you can, please buy organic. Not all foods are contaminated and it is very hard for you to know, but keep a watchful eye and be open to it. And as you know you can test these foods yourself using muscle testing [a simple process taken from Kinesiology, which by-passes the conscious, conditioned mind to reveal the 'truth'. This is what David Hawkins – see note 72 – uses in his work] and asking the body is it good for you? You have done this many, many times. And this is one way where you can know if this food is particularly good. It is at the moment mainly fruits that are being contaminated with chemicals. So

21

just beware. Also cereals, just be careful on the cereals, again additives are being put into these. Again you need to check them by muscle testing or any other ways you may have. Check these to test whether they are right for your body. Check rice in particular. Rice[7] is being contaminated, purposely so. Rice feeds hundreds of thousands of people and this is an easy way to get at the mass of the people all over the world. All countries are affected.

It is very difficult for you to make these choices; I just ask you go with your own intuition when you feel and hold these foods. You will know instantly whether they are good for you.

We will be talking for a few more sessions about breathing and how breathing has an effect, and how the breathing can help you with the healing.

Some of our healings that we are teaching and learning ourselves are from very ancient times and will be brought through to you, all in good time. If you could only see what we can see, even though it saddens our heart to know what is going on in your world, we also know there is a new dawn, and it will be dawning. And if you could see that, it would lift up your hearts. Yes, the old ways will crumble and people will be shown for what they are, and people will once again start to give, and start to care for each other.

In a world where it used to be so long ago, with no competition, no fighting, no wars and we are working on this so closely here up in the Heavens. And just be aware of everything that is going on around you. And lift your hearts up; even though sometimes it may feel very dark, keep going on and lifting your hearts up. The vibrations have to be raised up as you are well aware. Time on Earth is not easy at the moment and we are all aware of that here. None of you has anything to fear. If you lift your vibrations and live in the light of Love then you will get through this practically unscathed.

Yes, I remember you were talking to your friend [8] about aliens. They have been here for thousands of years without most of you being aware. They will make themselves available to your eyes. Some people are already able to see them.

[Are] crop circles[9] encoded? Yes they are indeed. But your governments will tell you lies about that. You will find there will be more crop circles coming. These are codes, and they are codes for the aliens that are helping you. The work that is going on is absolutely incredible.

So, I leave you with this. Lift up your hearts, lift up your hearts to the sun. Carry on, do the good work, spread the word as fast and as easily as you can. We are all here behind you, helping every one of you on the planet. We will gather more and more, people will come to you and you will know that they are from the Essenes. And you will work separately and sometimes you will work together. These things you will know as you meet these people. You will feel their vibrations and you will know that you have been with them in a previous life in the Essenes. And in many, many more lifetimes together, before and after. But we are all coming together now; the time is for coming together and lifting the vibrations of your planet at an incredible speed at an incredible time.

I will close with you now and say good night.

Diana contacted me a couple of days ago and was quite keen to let it be known that her bloodline was from the Essenes, and that Jesus was an Essene. She was very proud of that. What she wanted to get across is that it was very different from the blood-

line she had married into but she was cautious about what she said because of the consequences for myself.

We will see what happens over the next few sessions. I know there's a lot of information that she wants to give me, and I know there's a lot of information she won't, because she wants to shield me from bad publicity. Diana had very strong words to say about the Royal Family, but she said that we'll just leave it there for now.

MARCH 29TH 2012

Welcome and good evening. As I spoke previously about the Essenes I want to clarify the situation. Some of you may not know who the Essenes were. The Essenes were people who lived thousands of years ago. They lived along the shores and by lakes and by rivers. They did not live in the city. They knew the magic of water, far more than just cleansing.

I was an Essene and so was Anne [Stewart], and many of the people you come into contact with now. The Essenes were mainly vegetarians, who tended their crops, and had one of the best irrigation systems ever known in the world. They were called the therapeutics and would travel around by boat or on foot to tend and to heal people around Egypt, Greece and Israel. They were around for thousands of years. They taught Love and they worked with Love from the heart. Their teachings of healing were a seven-year process. They would pray to the Father, to God three times a day. They worked with the body; every organ of the body was worked through with nature.

For instance, the circulation system, the blood. They would imagine this was pure water running from pure rivers, and this was purifying the body, and purifying the blood. They would contemplate on this morning, noon and evening.

What is the importance of me telling you about the Essenes at this moment in time? Many, many Essenes agreed to incarnate 70-75 years ago. So at this moment and in these next few years, they can bring Love and light that is needed on this planet. You will all notice, and Anne certainly has, that certain people she is meeting here in the UK, and in Greece, are Essenes. On her last visit, Anne knew instantly that Vasiliki[10] had been an Essene. They talked about this, and Vasiliki realised too she had these qualities.

We are bringing these people back together now to start the new times for you. These people stretch back thousands and thousands of years. And their bloodline is pure. Their bloodline was so different to the bloodline I married into.

So, I want you now all to be aware. And as you talk to people, you will know and you will feel you have been with them before. Their healings were just wonderful and some of the [Essene] teachings I will be bringing to you the next few times we meet together.

Over the years, with wars and with the changing of the words in the Bible [11], the Essenes just faded out. But they are now coming back to be one again with mankind and humanity. And to make this place a better place. Working totally from the heart. So you will have freedom, you will have Love, you will have choice. More choice than you have now. You may think you have choice but you have very little. Very, very little. And the choices are getting less and less each day. Look around you. Be aware; things are not what they seem to be.

You are being hurried like sheep. Sheep into a pen. To be stamped, to be owned, and to be used. So come out of your hiding places.Face the sun. Face what's here for you; your life will be so much better. You will never, ever want go back to your old ways.

Okay Jack I believe you have some questions.

Thank you. Anne has, as you would expect, been met with sceptics who keep asking her for proof that you are Diana. Self-

evidently Anne, myself and many of our friends know that you are.
And neither of us are interested in gossip about your life on Earth.
One positive sign that is useful to us is that, once, I noticed Anne's
eyes change colour to cornflower blue.[12] *I just wonder if there are*
any things we can use to convince people that this is genuine?

You have noticed that Anne's eyes change to my colour cornflower blue, and very gently her face changes as well. I know about scepticism. I lived my life with the media. I lived my life in total torment. Whatever I did, the media jumped on me. The only time that the media were kind to me was after my death. We will not take Anne into any areas that she cannot cope with. We will be with her all the way. As I said previously, there are many things I could tell you, many things about my life that could be checked, and not checked. But I tell you this: over the next few years things will come to light that have been buried about my death. People will come forward who can no longer live with themselves. Who knew all about what happened to me and Dodi. And then it will be left for the world to judge. To judge those people who have question marks above them.

I'm not here to judge people any more; we have work to do. Humanity is more important to me than people of a lesser, lower vibration. And believe me there are a lot of them about. That is not our work. That is not of interest to us. For years and years the planet has just gone down and down and down. And now we have a chance to make everything so much better for everyone. I am not here to give people gossip. I am not here to tell people their fortunes; although I will help people if people are in distress, or they need some answers. I will do my very utmost to answer them.

My goal and my work here is, as it was on Earth, to help people. To help them realise their own potential. To guard them and to make them prepared. And to look around them, and to be aware. And to go one step forward, time by time, into the promised land. The land that should have been yours and mine aeons ago. The land that was taken and stripped from us. And the time has come now to take that back, to take our birthright and our birthplace back. It won't be done with wars. What are the wars doing? Killing with young soldiers. What is that achieving? Nothing for the people. That cannot continue, and it will not continue. People are seeing through it and are getting sick to the back teeth of seeing coffins come back and people being shot. We were never created for that as you well know. But people have to wake up and this is a wake-up call.

Anything else Jack?

Thank you Diana that was wonderful.

There is so much more that I could say, but I am not here to do that. And I don't want to put anybody in jeopardy. My life was in jeopardy and there are times I could have taken my own life, as you well know, or maybe you don't know? Because I know neither of you really followed my life, and that's good. That's good. And as you know, both of you have had problems with anxiety and depression and this is the path. Because, as your work continues, and you get busier and busier, you will find that the people that you will draw to you are so desperate. And it is through your own experiences, even though at the time it was pretty horrific for you… God never gives you more than you can handle, even though at times you will be taken to the brink. You had to go through these experiences as you well know, and you have come to this conclusion yourselves anyway, because people you are dealing with, and will be dealing with more in future, are of a disturbed nature. And, until people can get their minds cleared and drop into the heart, they are going to continue with depression and anxiety. And, as you know, that will be followed by physical illness.

The work you are doing with the Healing Code is absolutely wonderful and Alex Loyd was guided by God – as you were – to work with the Codes and to befriend Alex and for Alex to befriend you.

Of course there will be more stuff coming through at a higher frequency. But for now the Healing Code are the main things you must operate with. We will be dealing with other energies, coming through in the weeks and months that follow, that you can use in conjunction with the Healing Code or separately as your wish may be. We will look back on ancient healings that go back into Essenes. I will be giving those to you. Having been an Essene, Anne already has these teachings encoded in her heart; they just need to be awakened, which will happen as time goes on.

We are doing it as patiently and as quickly as we can, but we do not want to overload Anne. But we do need to get this message out, and it is very important. Just go with it, and know we will not put you through more than we know you can cope with.

Thank you and that leads me onto another question. You mentioned the last time you were with Anne about the simplicity of the healing approaches we use and ones no doubt you will inform us of. Is there any way we can overcome people's reluctance to accept something that is so simple, as we all know that is the only way we can succeed.

Well. Let me tell you, there is so much work going on behind the scenes for all of you that are on the right path. And I think in the next few weeks, doors, Heavenly doors will open, and people will become more awake, and more aware that it doesn't have to be difficult to heal. Simplicity is easier and better. Yes, do your work, and doors will start to open for you. Doors, I think, possibly you had never dreamed of opening. The Heavenly Spirits are working alongside you and, although I know times have been pretty tough. There were reasons for that. And reasons, that I think you know, so that we could get on this path. The path will now get easier for you. Doors will open. You will find people will come to you. Do your work and, as you have talked about specialising in depression and anxiety, that is the way we want you to go at this moment in time. Work with these people because, if they don't get their minds right, then nothing else will go right for them. And they will just end up with deeper and deeper depression. And, as we know, there will be suicides; some people will not be able to tolerate what is going on in the world. They will not be able to cope with the new energies that are coming in, and yes unfortunately people will take their own lives.

Thank you Diana. You mentioned Greece before, and as you know we have a very strong affinity to Greece, and we intend to move there. Anne noticed when she was walking round the [Acropolis] museum in Athens an amazing likeness between [a picture of] Diana or Artemis[13] and yourself. Do you have any connection to Artemis, is that one of your previous incarnations?

30

Yes, I have been many, many things. Many, many incarnations. And yes I was connected to her, as I was also connected to Atlantis. As you two realise we have reincarnated since the day we incarnated! We have had many, many lifetimes. With many, many things to learn. All of my lives were not so wondrous. And, as Princess Diana, my life was not wonderful. There were times my life was hell. My life was so lonely, and sad, fearful and so many emotions as I speak on this, but I always had my two boys to keep me going. I can understand how people who are depressed do commit suicide. I was there many, many times and the thing that kept me going was the Love of my two sons. Suicide isn't a way out. It wasn't for me but I can't say that, for some people, it may be their way out.

Again thank you for that answer. There are many things to ask you but I'm convinced, by what you said a few days ago, that all this will just unfold anyway.

Yes, but as I have already said we will not give Anne too much to cope with. My visitation to Anne last year in July was a shock to her but she knew that it wasn't her imagination. It was a shock and this doesn't happen to everybody. And, at the time, her mind was quite fragile but we needed to make that connection at that time. And, as you know, some very good friends of yours had already suggested someone would be at this house waiting. Had we told her who it was, you would never have believed it. And then we would not now be having this conversation. So we in Spirit, have to play it our own way, in the way that we knew would be acceptable. And yes it is a number of months now, but it will accelerate, and the book will go ahead, and there will be many, many teachings from this. It will be simple, but it will get out to people, and people will trust you. People already do trust you, and this is one of the reasons I chose Anne. Of course I had been with her in other times, and that was a great advantage. But I've seen the way you two were working, and I saw how people were so trusting of you, and how people would travel more than you ever knew to come and see you to have that privilege of being with you. I think you totally underestimate how people feel about you. And that's OK. But now it's time to spread your wings and no longer hide your light under a bushel. To go out there and feel free to deliver this stuff. Yes, there will be the sceptics, but I think you will be amazed. There will be less than you actually think. The media couldn't write any worse things about Anne or me or you Jack than was ever written about me when I was alive on the Earth plane. I was blamed for everything with the Windsor household. Perhaps the less said about that the better. This could get you into trouble so we will leave that as it is. This is not the time or the place.

Thank you again Diana. Just one last question. At times it was almost impossible to cope with Anne and yet I felt I was drawing on reserves of strength. At the time I felt it was my reserves of strength but I feel in a very different way to Anne I am guided, perhaps guided intellectually. I find connections, doors do open for me; but I just expect things to happen and it does. I wonder if there are any insights you can give me as to how that occurs?

I should have mentioned earlier, when I was talking about the Essenes, which was a little stupid of me, but I'm trying to get so much out, that Jesus was also an Essene. Anne knows I work a lot with Jesus; there are times when Anne is doing a healing I will be there with Jesus. And as you know Jack, you draw on the strength of Jesus. I think in the past you would have been reluctant to admit that, but you are opening up quite a lot now. But it is the energy of Christ that helped you through that. And also other Spirits. You have so much help from Spirit, so much help from your parents, from Gladys and Jack and Anne's parents. They are constantly around you. And Spirit world will never ever let you down. Sometimes we have to push you to the edge to get you to take that extra step. Without that, it would be easier [for you] not to do it. It certainly takes us out of our comfort zone, that's for sure. It would be a lot easier to just step back. Spirit needs people like you, and we need more people like you. The more that you train people, and the more you go around the country, then this work and this Love that you are teaching and are giving out will grow. And you will be amazed.

Thank you again Diana. You may or may not know, because Anne is far more familiar with the world of Spirit than I am, that whenever I do the Healing Code work there are always two people who come into my mind, Jesus and yourself. Every time. I thank you for that.

We are always around, and as you know in the last few weeks I have linked up with Harry [Edwards], who has been Anne's Spirit guide for many, many years, and he is just one wonderful man. Without Harry, people like him, and people like yourselves, we would still be in a very dark place as regards healing and the Spirit world. He was someone who took this forward, and not without his trials and tribulations. He did wonderful work. I am so pleased and so privileged to work with this beautiful man, whose energies are so wonderful.

And since I have been here in Spirit, I have met so many people of such high vibrations. And those who [we] would call just ordinary everyday people whose hearts and Love have just overwhelmed me. And the Love that they have for me. It is just so comforting to know all the people in Spirit who are helping me, and I can come through and help the likes of ourselves. Working with Harry and Jesus and, of course, we do work with Mother Mary. I know that Anne has visitations from Mother Mary, and these will become stronger. Mother Mary and I are connected as you know, through the Essenes. The Essenes were the most beautiful people I think this planet has ever known. They worked with animals, with plants and nature; worked from the heart, and were just so kind. But of course time came, and certain bloodlines wanted the Essenes out of the way, because they were doing too much good work. And so eventually, they were faded out. They have waited a few thousand years, but there are many, many people now who have reincarnated and have the souls and the hearts of the Essene people. And you will see more and more of that, and you will meet more and more people. Sometimes you will work separately, but over the next 12 months, you will gather together. And once you gather together in groups of 12, 24, 30, 40 or 50 and more, you will find the energy of that will just be awesome.

Have you time for one more question?

Yes.

As you know, one of my fascinations is to help people awaken. And there is no greater pleasure in helping people awaken through healing, which was Harry Edwards's goal. He articulated this in one of his books, and I find this so motivating. But there are other people who are not healers- David Icke[14] for example – who are helping people awaken. What is your view on people like him and others?

I think David Icke is something that was desperately needed. I liken myself to David Icke in many ways. That might sound quite strange to you because, of course, we seem like very different people. I came from a privileged background but my goal was to wake people up in a different way. David Icke, like me, suffered tremendous stress and torment. I admire and salute that man, for all that he has done, and for all he has given up so that he can bring the truth out; the truth that has been buried for so long. Hundreds and thousands of years this line of lies and deceit [has carried on], and this would have carried on without the likes of David Icke, and of course the Internet. The Internet is a wonderful tool, because no more do you need to be alone. People can get together and they can communicate with each other. Yes, there is a dark side, we know about that, but looking on the lighter side, David Icke and people that you know about, long may they go on. And long may they give out the truth. There is so much that I know, that I learned, that I wouldn't say at the moment, the time is not quite right, but David Icke has dug [up] the dirt, and long may he continue.

Thank you Diana I have no more questions.

There are so many good people on the Earth at the moment and, as you know, the work that you and lots of other people are doing will balance out, will tip the balance of the planet. There are many hundreds of thousands of you. Remember that. More need to awaken, but it is happening, and a lot of work is being done on this side and, as you know, most things are unseen. The work that the angelic beings are doing, the hierarchy are doing, Spirit world is doing here. If you were on this side you would feel so proud and honoured as we are going forward to take this planet into another dimension. And nothing will stop them.

But we need the likes of you and more people, to spread this out. So we can change, once and for all, the ugliness that has been going on for so long. I will leave you now. Thank you; it has been a privilege once again. We are going forward as quickly as we can.

CHAPTER FOUR

APRIL 2ND

Good evening and welcome. It's good to be back again with you. I want, today, to speak about anxiety and depression that is happening in your world. We are saddened here in Spirit to see all the troubled souls. They desperately need help and this is where you can come in to your own.

I know, from my own experiences, what it is like to have anxiety and depression. For not very long after my marriage to Charles I knew things were not going as they should. I knew at that time I would never be the wife of the King. And I would not be able to help Charles with the royal duties. As time went on it became more obvious to me about the third person. This took me into a spinning deep, deep depression. Which was hard for me, never having had it, to understand. And you must realise that I was in the public eye, so to speak it was a lot more difficult. And the media's eyes were always on me.

I know from the times I spent in the deep dark places, and my heart goes out to all those people on the Earth plane that are feeling those vibrations now; that you think you are all alone. And, in fact, you are alone because you retract into a shell. And you only have a very few close friends you can confide in. And, in my case, it was even more difficult because of the people I could trust. There were two or three very close people. Paul [Burrell] was one of them. And, later on, a very good psychic friend of mine. And a couple more people.

But as time went on, I got sicker and sicker. I couldn't eat, then I would eat. I couldn't eat, then I would eat, then I would be sick.

The thought of everything that was happening to me from being 19 years old and walking down the aisle with Charles, having my whole life ahead, just came to a black stop. The fear was, well, certainly I couldn't describe the fear that I had, and also the fear I had for my children. I thought I may lose my children because of the power of the Crown. So, night by night, I struggled on. Yes there were suicidal thoughts, I can't deny that. And then I would have to go out and do my duty. Sometimes I didn't know what I looked like. I would stare into the mirror, but when you are so depressed you don't see anything but the black thoughts.

And I have to laugh because Jack used to call me the clothes peg, sorry the clothes horse.[15] And I can realise why because when I looked at some of the photos of me when I was thin, so gaunt, so ill, that is exactly what I was. The clothes would just fall off me. I would go out and do these duties and be physically sick, knowing that the eyes of the world were on me. Knowing how dreadful I looked.

My main aim was to do the speech and get back into my darkness as quickly as I could. And it went on for a long, seemingly endless, time.

I remember one night in June, I can't remember the year at the moment, when I pleaded with God that I didn't want to wake up the next day. I pleaded that he would just take my life. That evening, I slept or I dreamt, or whatever happened, I felt I was being lifted up from my bed by Angels. I honestly thought at the time I had died. I thought that my prayers had been answered. I don't remember too much but I do remember being lifted up by six or eight angelic beings. And then I must have fallen into a very deep sleep.

I awoke the next morning feeling very different. I could see, through the little gap in the curtains, light coming through. Well, the sunlight had always been there but I had never seen it; I had never wanted to see it. And so, step-by-step, very gently, I began to feel better. I began to regain my strength with the help of two very good friends. I began to eat; I began to regain my self-respect and my confidence. And though it took a little while, I became to know myself again. And maybe I became a little rebellious at that time.

As time went on I devoted my thoughts, as I had always done in the past but this time in different ways, to children and to the landmines. And I knew then that I could help people. That made my heart soar; knowing that because of the position I was in [that] what I did would give credence and help and power. And, of course, to do these jobs we needed money. Because I helped and put my name to a number of causes, two in the main – one was the hospitals and the other was the landmines – the money came in. We were able to do a lot of excellent work. Not me in particular but the aides that I had working with me and for the causes. Through that is where I got my happiness and my Love.

So, I would say to anyone who is suffering an in-depth darkness, suicide is not the best option; there always is a glimmer. I know that once I had connected back to my Spirit realm, once I had connected back into God, the Creator, my life started to change around. There are many, many stories about this happening to people. Because when we are upset and unhappy, we just cut off from our source. Our source is with those from the day we are born and is with us until the day we die. Our source, our higher self, our Angels are there with us to help and guide us. But we have to evoke, we need to ask. Once we ask, sometimes overnight, sometimes it may take a little bit longer, but I promise you, surely things will start to change in your life. You will find your path. So never give up. Never ever give up. Just keep going on and on and on, doing what you need, helping others, sending Love to others, blessing and praying for them, praying for yourself and being at one with source.

You will notice that once you start to do this, and gather some good friends around you, your life will take on a totally different role; doors will open, Angels will open them for you, your path will be straighter. Even if you take tiny, tiny steps it does not matter; nobody is watching, nobody is waiting, only you. Only you, to be guided with the Love and light of God. And once you are there, things will start to happen. Know that you are a creation of God, and know that God counts every hair on your head. And you are never alone, never alone in the kingdom of God.

So lift your hearts and go forward; know you are special, very, very special, and know you are loved by all the angelic beings, all the Spirit beings, and the Creator.

I would like now to talk about meditation. It helped me such a lot. Because meditation quietens the mind, it aligns you with your source. And remember, be still and know you are God.

In the stillness everything happens.

So take time, even if it's only one or 2 minutes a day, build it up, sit with beautiful music and think of lovely thoughts. Beautiful scenes, the animal kingdom, a beach, the stars. And in a very short while be with God. Apart from connecting to your spiritual home, meditation has such wonderful benefits for the body and the mind. It frees the mind from the chatter, if only for a minute or two. Also, with the body, it helps with the heartbeat and the heart rate. It helps with the circulation in the body and blood. It helps the lungs. It has an effect on every organ. Because every organ is bathed in the Love and light of God. And every organ is slowed down and given a chance to regenerate itself. And, in particular, the immune system. It gives the immune system chance to bring back life into itself, to be able to breathe, to bring in the life force of God.

When we are rushing around or in an anxious state there is no energy left for the immune system. So it gets depleted. And, in time, if this carries on it cannot fight the bacteria, viruses and you yourself then become rundown and have colds and headaches. Which leads further on to other things.

There are various stages of meditation and you can go much further. The meditation I'm telling you is very simple. Once you start with this, you will feel the benefits very, very quickly in your body and in your mind.

When things get too heavy or too hard, ask help from your Angels, your higher self and from God. You will always get help. Always.

And so I leave you with that for tonight. You are all on a wonderful journey and sometimes I know it gets hard being in this material world. But you are doing so well and things are changing. I keep saying to you, it appears to be one step forward and two steps back, I assure you it's three steps forward. We can see this here in Spirit, but we are helping you. So just go forward, lift your heart to God, lift your face to the sun and be at one with yourself.

I will leave you now. Love to you all and blessings to you all, Diana.

CHAPTER FIVE

APRIL 5TH

Anne: *The last few days have been quite interesting. On Tuesday afternoons I work at Well Warrington[16] with people who have mental health problems. One of the ladies wanted spiritual healing. While I was doing the healing, I felt a very strong presence of Diana. She became clearer and closer and closer to me until, almost, she actually integrated within me. This is something I haven't experienced with her before. She hadn't been as close. Since then, that has happened a number of times. She is with me, I won't say constantly, but quite a lot, and I understand this is to push things along a little bit further. This morning while we were going to Manchester – Jack was driving – she came into my energy and I was given a healing symbol.[17]*

I had a client today, we were going to talk on Skype, but she rang me and said she wasn't very well. The lady is blind actually, and she is going to ring next week. I asked her if she wanted me to do some distant healing and she said she would. So I used the new symbol on her. I won't know the outcome of that until next week. But I felt the power of it, and there are certain areas the symbol goes on. I just want to try this out and see what happens.

What Diana is saying to me, and again this is me talking not Diana, is that my healing energies are beginning to change and get much stronger so that Spirit can work with me faster to get the message out.

Thank you, it is great to be back yet again. Tonight I want to talk very briefly about the angelic realms. At some stage, we will talk about this in greater depth.

I want you to be aware that the Angels now are very close to the Earth, more than they have been in thousands and thousands of years. They are coming to help; they are coming to guide you. Do not be afraid to ask for their help. They are waiting to be asked, to be invoked, in any way you want to communicate with them.

The Angels are more powerful than people think. They are God's messengers, sent by God on to the Earth plane and into your energies. They will help you in many, many ways. Their energies are beautiful, beautiful and gentle. But do not be mistaken; they are powerful beyond belief.

At the moment they are nearer to the Earth because of the way the Earth is and because human beings need our help and the guidance from Spirit and from the angelic realms. God knows what you need and He is sending all his workers out to help you all. All you need to do is shine; shine these lights and open up people. Once people are opened up, and once we can see [here] in the Spirit world the tiny, tiny dots of light on your dense, dark planet we can come in and help and work with you.

So much – as I keep saying – is being done here. And we know the pains that you are going through, but keep going on, as I have said many, many times because the corner will be turned. The Angels can help with anything. They can help from simple things if you just lose something, to you being ill or depressed. Just call in your Angels. I must stress, that once you have asked or received, please give thanks and gratitude to these wonderful beings. The more you do this, the more Love and light will open you up. These beings bring messages of God to you, and take your messages back to God. And don't think they are not being worked on if things don't happen immediately. Sometimes we just have to have time and patience for God and the Universe to work out the best way for you to have the best.

While I am talking to you now I can feel the energy, of every energy criss-crossing. The energy goes in spheres, in circles, in spirals, in never ending spirals. It goes in orbs. In so many ways does energy reach you and come to you from our world and from the Universe. We are all connected. We are all connected to the animal world, to the stars, to the sun, to the moon. Everybody here on Earth and in other galaxies are all connected. It is like fine threads of gossamer throughout. It is quite amazing to see how all this works, and how everything is so ordered here in the Spirit world, and although you may think it is chaos, and chaos in your world, actually it is all ordered and working for your best ends. The fine layers of ether, the fine layers of gossamer that you are unaware of, but some psychics and clairvoyants can see them, are layers and layers of beautiful fine energy; etheric energies. While you are asleep, and while you are resting, these energies come down from God's Heavens and help to heal and cleanse you. There is so much going on in your world that you are so unaware of. But that's fine because it is up to us here in Spirit world to help and to heal you until, one day, when your minds become clearer, and when you connect, when you can see more with your third eye, then you will see all these beautiful things that we see.

Do not be troubled in this time. Just know in your heart everything is working fine. New energies are coming in, new things are happening, and everything is going so fast now it is almost like a spinning top. That is how it's meant to be. Everything is working to plan. So just relax and know over the next few weeks and months, things will change, and you will all feel better. The aches and the pains and the headaches, the feeling of faintness and the dizziness will all disappear. As the finer vibrations come into your body they will clear out the old, stagnant beliefs that have been there for so long.

I will say to you please drink plenty of pure water. This will help to take away the toxins as the new energies come in and the old energies go out. It will help to vibrate the body at a higher level. None of this is complicated; all of it is quite simple. All you need to do is just trust, and just know that God is working for all of you. We are all working for all of you. The angelic realms are working for all of you.

Just go one day at a time and see how everything unfolds for you. Life is an ever-increasing circle, but a beautiful circle.

And if you could just see the colours that I'm seeing now, that in itself would lift you to the height of Heaven. The colours of the beauty that surround you, if only you could see them. And, in time, you will. When you are unblocked from all this negativity, when you can see and feel things and be far more sensitive than you are now [you will see them]. And it doesn't happen overnight. But you can work on it and we are working with you.

So until we meet again, just remember: use your breathing to relax, take pure water, and be at one with God and the Universe.

Long pause…

The spirals of light, as I try to close this session, are so beautiful. I just wish I could just transfer them and let you see them. I'm finding it very difficult to close and go back down to spirit because the vortex here, that we have set up, is just too wonderful to leave.

I must go and I will return again. God bless you all, I Love you all, and we will speak again soon.

Anne: *It was hard to come out of that then.*

CHAPTER SIX

APRIL 8TH

Happy Easter and thank you for inviting me here today. I used to love Easter when I was on the Earth plane, for many reasons.

The main [reason] is that I could play with Wills and Harry and we would run around hiding Easter eggs. We could do that for hours on end; we used to have great fun. Such happy, happy memories.

But the other [reason], also when I was on the Earth plane, is about new beginnings. To see the blossoms, to see how God can turn the seasons, and how the seasons just happen? No, the seasons don't just happen. We think they do but there is so much intelligence that goes on as these plants go deep within the Earth during the winter months, and know exactly when to come out and when to flower, when to fruit. And that is all because they trust in God. They can do anything, they can just nurture themselves. Feed from the soil, from the Earth and just wait and trust in God Almighty. Who never, ever lets them down.

Easter here in the Spirit world is magnificent. We have beautiful flowers and blossoms so wonderful your eyes wouldn't be able to see them. So magnificent are the colours. We also celebrate with angelic singing, something you could never, ever imagine on your plane. And beautiful celebrations, of praising to God in the highest, God Almighty, for all the wonderful gifts He gives to us all. And we should give gratitude for even the smallest things because they are given to us every day of our lives. Every day of our lives we are given things; we are given food, we are given water, the air that we breathe, beautiful friendships that we have with one another.

Never, ever doubt those friendships because that is what living on the Earth plane is all about. Giving Love to each other, helping each other, having a very good close circle of friends that we can talk to and share. And I would say to you all, in this moment and in this time, mix with people of your own likings, mix with people that will hold your higher vibrations. Make your circle of friends on the same level as you are, so that you can discuss what is happening on the Earth. And instead of getting despondent, [they] can lift your hearts up.

I know that yesterday Anne and Jack were healing, and were running a course.[18] And I was there, on the odd moment I would just fleetingly pop in. The energies in that room were absolutely magnificent. And those people now will go out and spread the Love and that healing that was being taught.

And we want to say to you that sometimes it isn't easy doing the work, travelling, trying to get people to the courses. We know that. But never give up; never feel down about it, because this wonderful healing that you are spreading is growing. And maybe you may not realise how quickly it is growing, and how many people are actually benefiting from the Love, the healing and the wellness they get from it all. And the trust they have in you as well, which is so important.

We need to care for each other and, most of all, we need to care for ourselves. Everything that seems to go on in your world seems to be chaotic; some of it is. But here in the Spirit world everything is orchestrated, everything is in order, and so it is in your world too, if you would just be aware. Yes, there is chaos, man-made chaos. But take your time, day by day and look at what happens each day for you, and start the day by thanking God for all the wondrous things that will happen to you.

Set your scene, set your boundaries and your hopes and, as you say that morning prayer, you will find energies in the body change. Because you have connected and asked God for guidance and help. And God never says no. He always says yes. And when you ask for help you will get it, and by saying that daily prayer, you are connected to guard and you are connected to Mother Earth.

And you will be able to tolerate the static, the noise of the outside world, and become not even aware that it's there, staying within your own inner self. Going within your own heart, asking the questions within. Because the questions are within and not out there. Nothing is out there. It is all within you. You create it all from within.

And you know we have said many times about your thoughts to try and keep them as pure and as kind to each other as you can. Because when you attack each other, if you could see the energy when vile words are spoken – that energy going from you to the other person – that energy attacks that person and can make them unwell. Truly, I can tell you what we give out on the Earth [plane] we will get back. It is like a boomerang. It may not [come back] instantly, but it will come back.

So, say your prayers, open your heart, think of beautiful things. And when you do that, it makes our hearts sing here in Spirit, because we know there is a change. And when you sing and when you are happy it filters up to the Heavens and the Earth, and it filters out into the consciousness. And by you smiling and being happy it has an effect on every person on the planet. And you might think that's strange to say 'everyone else on the planet', but it really does. And that is why, when you do your healing, and you have your small groups, just be aware [that] the power that is going out is unbelievable.

If you could see the power and the energy that goes out when you have groups of 10 or 12 – obviously if it's bigger it's even better – the power that ripples out into everyone else is just magnificent for us to see here in the Spirit world. Because, as you are sending these loving energies out, dark energies that are around you are changing. If you could see the colours that are in them, the beautiful lilacs, the vibrancy of the indigo colours, of pinks and greens, all colours here that we have in Heaven and the Spirit world…how these colours change, and change the negativity on the planet. So go out and do your work and spread this wonderful, wonderful healing.

And everything is attuned to each other and in tune with each other. The moon affects the moods, so do the tides, and the sun. And the information we get, the information that is coming through from other galaxies to help us and to give us strength and to give us communication. Communication like it's never been in our lifetime, and that's a wonderful and absolutely fabulous thing to happen. Because you can communicate with the four corners of the Earth, you can communicate with people you may never, ever meet and they with you. And we can spread all [these] wonderful, wonderful teachings, of yours, and Alex's and all the other wonderful people doing the work on the healing, and with the psychics and mediums.

And there is so much more coming in, it's almost like strands of information, coming through to you. The healing that both you and Jack are doing, both of you are going to have new energies, and you will feel them. Over the next 2 to 3 weeks, both of your energies will change. We're doing this very subtly and very gently – because it can affect the body – we want it to affect you as [gently] as possible. We know you have work to do, and the writing of the book, and the Diana workshops are now important and the time is right to get this information out. We said here in Spirit we would drip-feed it out, and we have done that, and we would give you information, and you have that information.

So now, over the next 2 to 3 weeks, shifts of energy will come into your body and your vibrations will get lighter and higher. It may be, and I don't want to say this and put thoughts into your head, it could be that you will feel these changes. But don't be alarmed because any little aches or pains will only be gentle; will pass very quickly. I do also want you both to meditate, and to put out into the world the Love you have in your hearts, and then we can take this journey forever and move it more quickly. I want to get it out into the world. I think that's all that there is for today. I think, Jack, you may have wanted to ask some questions?

Thank you Diana. For the first time I would like to say how much it is a privilege to be part of this whole process. I've just been glimpsing at other books written by people who have communicated with you and channelled your words. Hazel Courteney and Rita Eide.[19] Those books are wonderful and I noticed in one of them that quite a lot what you are now sending through to Anne is similar. I'm just wondering how this will be positioned in a way that is perceived as different? I know there is more emphasis on healing with this particular channelling, which is wonderful for us, but I'm wondering if you could comment on other people who have published the channelling that you have had with them and how that lies with Anne?

Well although there may be similarities, this is very different. Each one that I have channelled through has been very different. Although, of course, as I say there is a lot of similarity because that was my life! That's how it was and we can't change that. But, as we go on this is healing, it has nothing to do with channellings that have been done before. This is about healing people, and helping people to heal themselves. Does that answer your question?

Perfectly. That is exactly what I thought. There is another question. I love the science behind this; I love to be able to explain a lot of what goes on, yet knowing that not all things are capable of explanation. Is this also helpful to people – I believe it to be – but I just wanted your reassurance on this, that we can explain some of the healings that we do based on some of the scientific explanations?

Absolutely. Everything is orchestrated for you, and I know you have been reading several books, and those books have come to you in various ways, and they are right for you to read now.[20] You see, for so long there has been mystery and mysteries around the healing, and the gurus. I know we laugh about the gold medallion but it actually exists with those who want to make it mystical; who want to keep it away from the everyday people. I want to get it out to the everyday people, these are the people that I Love and these are the people [who] need the help. Why should it be just for the few? No, no, this is what we want you to do [said with emphasis]. We want you to explain it, in the way that they will know in simple ways. Make it simple. The healing is simple. It always was. I know Anne was watching King of Kings[21] and felt very moved because a lot of stuff resonated with her, because of course we have been in times like that together, and it was simple. When we were Essenes it was simple. Sometimes you only had to touch people and they would be healed. You didn't have to have a load of hocus-pocus to go with it. All that does is feed the mind. We don't need that.

And yes, some people will like all the add-ons, and all the bits and that's fine. But they will come around eventually to realising that they don't need it. They just need the pure Love and the pure intention, the purity from each other's heart.

You know I'm sure that you both wonder sometimes why this has happened to you. And why it has happened in the way that it did. We know it has been very unpleasant in some ways for you but we needed somebody; we needed people who were pure of heart who could take this message through, who people would trust and love. And that's why you were chosen.

We have to get this message out. You have to get it out to people who would trust you, and you would be amazed how many people do trust you and want to work with you. And we know sometimes it can be a bit overbearing, a bit bewildering even, a bit, 'well is this real?', am I going mad? Know you're not going mad. I know what going mad is, I had that on the Earth plane, and you are not going mad. But it is different. And we chose you because we know you will carry this through, you will do this work for us, and you will be able to train many, many more people.

So yes, you talk about the morphic field[22] and that is what we are doing. This stuff will get out; you will teach other new teachings and other new healings to people. I want to say you will teach some to the masses. Although you may not be able to see this and understand this now, it will happen.

And it will change the world.

Does that answer your question Jack?

You will forgive me for being slightly emotional, of course. I'm almost at the point that I can anticipate what you're about to say. I have expected this all my life, I have known for decades, but not known how it would manifest of course. I just thank you again. That's all I can say.

It is my greatest pleasure and I also know that Anne, from the day she was born, knew that she would teach healing. And never knew how it was going to come about. And it didn't come about in the way she thought, where there would be a transition from one to the other[23] – that could never be. It would have felt better for her and you. That could never be. It needed a jolt to take you to another level. Another level of awareness. You know now that your awareness is going so quickly, you are learning so many new things, and this will all come together. And it will be wonderful for everyone who you come into contact with.

And I know that a number of your dear, close friends have told you these things, and yes it does seem hard to believe when your world has practically been turned upside down. But visualise it every day, and the new energies will come in fairly quickly. You do have a lot of work to do but we know you can do it. Sometimes you might have to rest more, and that doesn't mean sleep. Maybe just put your feet up, play beautiful music, meditation, silence. Because it's only in silence that we meet God, and know God.

It's only in silence that you meet me, and Harry, and Jesus. And our three energies are now binding together to come and help you. Your power will be so empowering to others but you will find you will be working more. But I know that won't bother you. Things will come easier, and things will change as they do. Sometimes you will think you haven't time for the next breath but you will have. And we will carry you. And sometimes it's hard to trust when the world is so mad at times and the noise is so shrill. You will find you will have to go and be quiet, because the noises of the world you will not be able to tolerate and you will need to be in your own peace. Maybe just in a wood, or sitting in a park.

You need to be in nature; you need that space. You need to be one with nature, watch nature, learn from it. Because, as nature unfolds so do you. You are unfolding, you are blossoming, and your blossoms will be full.

And we want to thank you here in Spirit world, because we know sometimes it is difficult when there [are] only a handful of people. But we know you will never let those people down, and those people will multiply and tell others. You are aware of this, but sometimes in the harshness of the world it is hard to think ahead, and visualise a gathering, a huge gathering of like-minded people. But your energies will attract these people, and you saw that yesterday. I know you saw that. Yesterday was very different energies, very different people. When you think you weren't going to do that at one point, and we thank you for doing that. It's your holiday time, it's your Easter time – and you didn't have to do that and we are grateful.

From that small gathering yesterday, you will be amazed at what comes from it. And that place, and Jan, and John and Sylvia are truly blessed.[24] I tell you this, truly blessed. And there will be more people coming to you like that, offering you places. I know you have already got one. People will be kind to you. They want to have you in their presence because when they are in your presence their energy lifts. And without knowing it you were…? As I'm saying this my heart is just growing so big with Love for you.

As I have said, there are no new teachings, this is not going to be a profound book in one way because what I'm saying has been known for millions of years. I'm just trying to put it in a way that people will understand it and get it out to the masses, because of how people loved me when I was on the Earth plane, and how much I loved them.

And so it is help from Spirit in the way we know so you can evolve and spread. I wish that you could be here, but not quite at this moment, here in the celestial realms because it is so quiet and peaceful. When I say peaceful, there is music, wonderful music, and Angels singing. The peace and the Love is something that I will bring to you and you will experience in time to come.

And remember Jesus's teachings of healing were so, so simple. There were no fluffy bits and dingly bits. It was just pure Love and the touching of the body. And what we will teach you is to connect very deeply into people's hearts. And the workshop will be about this deep connection, and the feeling of Love from Spirit. And the feeling of Love from me. Because I will be with you, as I am anyway. But I will be with you on every one of these workshops. People will feel my presence, and people will have a wonderful change in energies. And they will go away feeling different, feeling empowered, and they will spread that word for you. And we will all do the work together.

We are determined here in the Spirit world to turn your beautiful world around. There will be people who are not ready for this yet, and that's fine. Because they have their journey too and they can't leap from one energy level to another overnight. It is all about stepping stones, and learnings and teachings as we go on our journey. And they will find their way eventually to where it is that they need to be. It doesn't mean they are any lesser than anyone else, they are just on their own journey. And just bless them and let them go on their way.

But I have said this before to you, about my plan, about my death. But I couldn't have helped the planet and humanity like I can as I'm here. I could have helped a few, but as I am here I can help many, many more.

And, as Anne knows, I do visit other people. I visit her friend Judith[25] and I give her information for Anne that we are here, we are here with her. Because it is a lot to take on board, but we orchestrated it well and it was step-by-step to where we are now. And if you look back on the last few weeks, we are immensely proud of how quickly you have taken the messages, and how quickly you are using those messages. Far quicker than we thought. And so we bless you here in Spirit, with Love in our hearts. And we thank you for all that you are doing.

I know that you are going out this evening to celebrate Anne's birthday. We bless you and thank you and know you will have a wonderful time. I know that families are important. I didn't have the family I thought I would have had. But I had my two wonderful boys who I watch every minute of every day. But I missed the family. I missed sitting round the table, I missed going out and being a family. That was taken from me, and that hurt, really hurt. So I say when you have families, know you are blessed.

I also know Jack that you are having a visit from your brother [Ray] [26] later this year, in May. I think you will find him very much like you; I think you will be pleasantly surprised. And you will find that you have a lot in common because, although he may not show it, he is quite a heart centred person.

Be aware, have an open mind, because we are sending you signs. And you just need to be vigilant, and all these coincidences that are happening, are not as you know coincidences, they are orchestrated from us here in Spirit.

I always find it hard to leave when I am here, but leave I think I must do, because Anne is getting tired and I know you have to go out this evening. So we will meet again very soon, and we thank you all from our hearts here in Spirit for what you are doing. God bless you.

APRIL 10TH

Welcome. I feel at home again here. It's been very busy here in Spirit with the celebrations and everything that has been happening. New beginnings of life, and the circles of life coming and going.

I want to talk to you tonight about God, the Creator, the Great Spirit. We have many names for God, but there is only one true God, call Him or Her what you will. And I want to tell you and confirm to you, that the God we have, the one and only God is a truly, truly loving God.

We listen to conversations here from you on the Earth plane and sometimes God is known as a fearful God, a spiteful God. That is never, ever true.

Some of the stories have been made up, some of the stories in the Bible have been changed, changed by mankind. God only wants the very best for you. And even when you feel you have let Him down, do not be afraid, you will not be punished, not by God. You will be helped, and you are still very, very much loved by the power and the Love of God.

People say, 'well why does God allow these wars?' God doesn't allow the wars, mankind does. God doesn't want war, God just wants you to be you; the beautiful human being that you were born to be.

Don't be frightened and scared by what you hear and what you see about God. God is your father; He wants the best for you. He is always striving to give you the very best of everything. Just look around you, in the springtime, the beautiful flowers, the blossoms will in many, many cases turn to fruits in the autumn for you.

God has thought of everything possible, for you and all his children and people here on the Earth plane. There is an abundance of everything. An abundance of food, an abundance of wealth. But we are told from a very, very early age that everything is in very short supply. There isn't enough food, there isn't enough money, there isn't enough Love. There is plenty; plenty of everything.

Open your heart to know that, and open your heart to know, in the very darkest hours, you are never alone because God is always there with you.

And people say, 'how can you talk directly to God?' We say, well why not? And people think they have to go through Jesus, or through Angels. These are God's messengers of course, you can speak directly to God. Anytime, anywhere. You don't have to wait for Sundays, the special day. God is always waiting to hear from you no matter what time of day or night. He waits with open arms to hold you in your hour of need. There doesn't have to be a special time. Where did that come from? Who made that up? No, I can assure you, God is always on hand, every minute, every second of your life, to communicate with you for the best. Because He wants to give you the best, you were brought into the world not to suffer, but to enjoy this life full of Love, full of beautiful things, full of plentiness.

As I'm here now I can see, I smile as I remember new-born chicks running around. What is more beautiful than a new-born chick? The breath of life, the breath of God, in that beautiful bundle of furry, feathery, yellowy, beautiful, beautiful thing. On two stick legs. But still very beautiful in their own small way. And the lambs, and the rivers and the trees, all full of everything for you. Everything has a purpose; nothing is wasted in God's world. Everything is recycled.

But I want you to know in this short message, do not be afraid of God, do not fear that if you do wrong you will go to hell. Part of our human experience is learning and sometimes we do wrong things. I know that, I did plenty, plenty.

God never, ever gives up on you. God always blesses you, and forgives, because we can learn from these things, and move on and grow in our spiritual way. In every one of us, in every one of our hearts, is that spark of God. We are all connected to God and we are all connected to each other. How can things go wrong in this reality when all you have is a loving God surrounded by beautiful, angelic forces, and wonderful, wonderful energy? What can go wrong when you are in this reality? And it is just a whisper away, all you have to do is just step into it. Feel the essence, feel the power. The power that you are.

When you think you are powerless, and can't move on and may be stuck, just connect to God and you will feel that wonderful power. And you are powerful beyond your own beliefs.

We are told from being small children that we have no power. That we have to do as we are told. And laws are laid down for us, and we adhere to them, and we become like puppets. Now it is time to break free of all this, free, and be at one with yourself and with your Creator, your source. The Godhead. Knowing that you are loved and cared for throughout your life.

Yes, of course you can pray, pray to God, pray to Jesus. Whenever you say your prayers they are heard and they are never, ever ignored. And the more of you that pray, the more the beautiful, beautiful energies will change. So do not be afraid to say your prayers. Say them in private, say them with each other, say them in the churches. Because the energy of that prayer has astounding effects on your world, and on our world too.

You know things can be changed by prayer; it is written in many of your books. Never, ever under estimate the power of just one short prayer. Simple, short and said with Love. That sort of prayer can move mountains, believe me. And we rejoice here in Spirit world when we hear you praying to God, and blessing the Angels. It lifts our hearts beyond belief, and know that we are all one and we are with you in every way. All you have to do is call us.

So remember, God isn't out for revenge, God only wants to Love you as we do here in Spirit world. And we send our Love and blessings to you this evening and know you are in our thoughts here in Spirit, always in our thoughts. We are always working towards your best and for your best intention.

There are many, many more things we need to say, but I think now we will just close this short session and more will be said about these things as we progress.

So blessings to you all, with all my Love we will speak again soon. Thank you and God bless.

Chapter Eight

APRIL 13TH

Well good evening; it's lovely to be here once again. I know that there have been races on, and I have been aware of what's been going on over in your Aintree[27] races. I want to talk today about how we treat animals, how we mistreat animals. Animal abuse, which is widespread.

Some of it I know is through ignorance, some of it is just through cruelty. I want you to think what the world would be like without all these beautiful creatures. How quiet, how silent, how it would lack the vitality of the horses and cattle and sheep in the field on a summer's day. Looking out into the field, dotted like little white specks, as you drive closer you see these are beautiful, living, breathing creatures.

How desolate it would be without the beauty of the animals in our countryside. Think about this. They are living energy just like you and I. Of course they have feelings and emotions, just like you and I. And when you have an animal, whether it's a horse, dog or a cat they become your true, loyal friends. They would never hurt you either physically or mentally. All they want to do is be by your side and share your life and your Love with you. And I know a lot of people do that with their animals. But there is still quite a lot of cruelty. And I ask you to be aware of this, and to me there is nothing more cruel than the way some animals are kept prior to slaughter.

Yes, you will eat your huge, juicy burger. But if you knew how those animals were kept you would spit it out very quickly. Some of those animals are kept in the most dire conditions you could ever imagine. Kept well away from our eyes, hidden, kept just to eat and to produce fat and meat. Most of the time induced by chemicals. And these animals live in total fear. They are like slaves, chained and fed and kept in the most unbearable conditions. Conditions that you could never, ever imagine.

Think, as you eat this food, it is full of chemicals, it is full of fear. Fear from the animal, fear in every cell of the animal's body. Fear in every part of the animal, fear in every organ. And you are eating that. And you wonder why there are so many cases of heart disease and cancer? Do you ever stop to think what you are eating, full of hormones, full of chemicals, full of fear? Look about you and see, check your food when you buy it and, if you are going to consume meat, do your very best to know how these animals have been kept.

Hens kept so close to each other they can hardly stand up. And in fact with broken limbs. There is no need to farm with such intensity, there is enough food for everybody. God has made sure of that and has provided, provided us with fruits and grains and berries. There is no shortage. It is just that we are told there are shortages.

In the late summer, when the apples are on the trees, a huge proportion of the apples and pears lie on the grass and on the ground. There is more than enough for everybody.

So I ask you to buy wisely, to check where your food is coming from, and to research how these animals are kept. These animals are a creation of God, just like you and I. And we are all connected. You may find that hard to believe; we are all connected, all one. So think and feel for these beautiful animals.

Also remember to keep yourself healthy. You need good nutrition. And some of this food is not nutritious at all. The opposite. So give a thought to the animal kingdom, see the richness of all the animals throughout the world. How sad it would be if all that was gone. God provides everything for us, everything to give us pleasure, everything to give us Love and compassion. And that's what animals do. So give that back and be kind to the animals that you meet.

We know that there are places where poaching and killing takes place for certain parts of animals; again these creatures are being depleted. We are very fortunate that there are people out there who care, who are providing shelter for these animals to make sure that the species will live on to give us pleasure. The beautiful cats, the rhinos, elephants, giraffes, [the list] is endless. God's work is endless.

Think about the butterflies on a summer's day. The birds. How silent it would be without the birdsong. The dragonflies, the ladybirds. We take all this for granted. But we have to care, because these are God's creatures and we have to share this planet. So educate yourself, read, watch your televisions, source the Internet and fill yourself with knowledge about these beautiful animals. You will find it most rewarding. Open your eyes and open your hearts and remember, and remember, always remember we are all one.

Do you have any questions?

Yes, thank you Diana. And just let me say as I read through this material and put it into the book how much it is starting to change me.

Great, good, I hope it has an effect on lots and lots of people.

I'm sure it will.

I just want to reach out from the heart and let people know there is more to life than the material world. We are surrounded by such bountiful beauty. If only they would just open their eyes and see it. I know it is happening, I see it here, we all see it here in Spirit. But then we are a little bit impatient, and I know we shouldn't be, but we want it to happen a little bit faster. Only because it will help you all on the Earth plane, and we only have your interests here in Spirit at heart.

One of the two questions I wanted to ask you. I'm sure you're familiar with Neale Donald Walsch[28], who is a hero of both Anne and myself. He used the expression 'Looking the other way while the train is coming' to describe those who ignore or turn a blind eye to the dark things that are going on. The problem I have personally is, how much do we talk about waking people up versus telling them to Love each other? It seems to be a difficult balance at times.

I'm not quite sure – there seems to be two different questions there? Just rephrase them.

How much attention do we put on waking people up by pointing out what's going on? You have just given the example of cruelty towards animals. We could talk about the greed of people who are currently running the planet, and all that kind of stuff; it is something that fascinates me. But I don't want to get the balance wrong; this is me personally outside of the book and your words. To place too much emphasis on waking people up, or stressing loving and caring for each other?

Well, I think the two are so close together. As people wake up, and come out of their own cocoon – and, dare I say it, selfishness in some cases – that once they do open up and are aware then, to me, they can only but open the heart. And realise that the only healing that will ever be done on the planet is through the Love of God. So I don't think there is any separation.

So it's okay to point out the realities of what's going on in the world and at the same time....

I don't see how it can be done any other way. You have to be honest. We have to be truthful about what's going on and I think there is a balancing. I think you know that intuitively. You will know how far to go and, again, it depends on the individual themselves as to how and where they are in their life.

There will be some people who will be very difficult to change, maybe that's because they're not ready and that they have to go through whatever it is they are going through for their next stage [in evolution].

All we do, and all you can do, is open that door slightly for them, for them to take the step. Does that help, does that answer your question?

It does, as it does always [laughs]. I have just one other question which is similar. When we were in Greece with our Essene friend Vasiliki, I was talking to her about how we promote the healing that we are doing and the stuff she is doing and her answer was quite unequivocal saying that we don't push it, we don't market it, we do it more through word-of-mouth. Perhaps in a more gentle way, that you are expressing through this book. My own view is that through this book and the workshops we are doing we don't need to push it down people's throats.

It has to be a gentle approach but you also have to let people know what you are doing and where you are doing it. It is putting it out into the thought field. We do have to take action, but the people want to, and the people who need to will find you. As I have said before this will grow. The work you are doing is excellent and you know the difference it is making to people's lives. The more you do, of course, the more it multiplies. Word-of-mouth. You know we send you the right people, send you people so that you can learn and of course they [can] learn. As long as you put the message out from the heart, people will find you. Is there anything else?

No thank you. I look forward to the next time you come and talk to us.

I know a lot of people are quite down in the mouth. They think that this so-called recession is never going to end. And some are losing faith, and some are finding it very hard to carry on. They feel there's just nothing at the end. Certainly, by the end of the year, in fact before the end of the year, things will start to change and people will feel a little more joy and happiness within them. There has been a lot of energy changing, a lot of work we've had to do. And, of course, there is a lot of negative energy around as you know; it has been around for so long now. We have to break through that, but it is happening, truly it is happening.

We thank you for the work you're doing and all the people you are in contact with that are on a similar journey.

Without the likes of yourselves and many thousands of others like you this would be an even harder journey. So know that we are travelling on, and cutting through the darkness.

And remember, Love and light will always win through in the end.

So tell your friends and people, do not be disheartened, changes are happening that may not be out in the open, or people may not be aware of what is happening, but it is happening. And we're moving on. Actually, we are moving on faster than we thought, so it is going to be a great time in the next year or so and things will change. And truths will be told and people will realise that they have been conditioned. But that conditioning can be changed very simply. People can start to live a happier and a fuller life. And the fear and the negativity that is surrounding the planet at the moment is dispersing.

And as more people give out their Love and care for each other, help the planet, the lighter energies will take over.

So it has been my pleasure to have been here with you again this evening. I look forward to the next time. Love and blessings to you all. We will meet again soon.

CHAPTER EIGHT

Chapter Nine

APRIL 16TH

Well here we are again, I am so excited. This day has been wonderful. We have seen the energies going into Anne and I know now, as we speak, her hands have been tingling and have been for the last 30 minutes or more.

We were really pleased this afternoon when you spoke to your friend Julia.[29] And you heard me say 'use the new symbol', and you did. I was so pleased that you did that and, as you know, Julia immediately felt so much better.

So the energies are changing as I promised you that they would 2 to 3 weeks ago. They are coming in really fast, they're coming in from all spheres. And I'm so excited, so excited I could hardly speak that we have someone who is joining us this evening, and it is your friend Harry, Harry Edwards.

Harry wanted to come and say hello to you and thank you for all the work you've been doing *[Anne is struggling to keep up*[30]*]*, for all the years you have worked with him. And allowed him to work through you.

We are coming together now to mass this energy for you. It is important and we have to get it out, but we have to time it right. And I did speak to you [about this] the other day; it cannot be rushed but I can assure you it is accelerating so fast that you won't know whether you are on your head or your heels. We are warning you, we will be with you, we will guide you but it's going to be quite a thing to happen.

Jack's energies will also start changing, and although he is feeling tired at the moment *[true!]* this is part of it. Energies are aligning with his body, and it does take time sometimes, and it does take it out of your human body.

Anne, I am so glad you got the minerals, and I suggest Jack starts taking some as well. *[Two days earlier, Anne had bought some calcium and magnesium tablets].*

The energies are coming in from every sphere, and it is just overwhelming for us, and so wonderful to know we have you to work through and we can bring on this new healing.

As you know now, on a couple of occasions you have used the new symbol. It's simple and that's how we want to keep it. Simple, simple, simple. We will help you all we can. The healing will be done mainly through the breathing, through the eyes and through the symbols. And we will go more into this as the days and weeks pass by. You will also notice there are a lot of the angelic forces around you.

We are bringing this healing from every dimension. This is ancient healing that has not touched your world for so long. This is why I wanted to work with you. We have done it gradually, and slowly, and now the time is coming very close. We told you we would drip feed it out to you and then it would go, and go it will. But don't worry, we are with you, we will keep this going and we will keep you going. It's all so exciting for us, we can hardly contain ourselves.

This will work wonderful with animals as well. *['This is giving me a headache' – Anne].*

We know the vibrations are very, very strong. We will try and tune them a little bit more softly for you. I know that you are feeling them through your body, through your hands and now through the rest of your body. This won't last forever, it will be a short time and then your energy levels will be so different. Your healing energies will be so different. I'm sure you have noticed over the last week or so they have become more intense and stronger.

We are starting to slow the energy down now for you, so that you can breathe better. I know that you are seeing Jayne[31] next week and she will see a vast difference from when she first met with you.

[The words are now coming through at about half the previous speed.] There are so many wonderful things we want to tell you, and I know you are feeling slightly confused because everything is coming in on you. Just let it filter through and take what you can from it, because we will give you all this information again and again. Take from it what you can.

Know at the moment you are connecting with other galaxies, drawing upon their energy. Thank you, that is wonderful that you can do that. See the beautiful colours that we see now, the purples and the indigos, the pinks, the violets, so bright. These are the colours that are being given to you. They have been aligned now with your body. Take time, breathe them in, see them filling your body. You are in such a different world now, we have transported you here.

You can see all the galaxies; it is [as] though you are flying slowly, so slowly through each and every one of these. So vast, we want you to be aware of how big and how wonderful everything is outside your world. And you, and all human beings, have help from these other galaxies. We will not let you fail, we will not let your planet [be] destroy[ed]. We are so pleased that we have been able to do this with you.

It is an immense obligation you have taken on, and I say thank you so much and so highly. We have pushed you, and pushed your boundaries, particularly tonight because we wanted to take you out so you could feel and encapsulate these energies that we wanted you to have.

Remember to use the symbol, it is so powerful and you will find that as you continue to use it.

You will find now that people will come to you from all different directions. We must ask you to take time out just to meditate, just to keep the energy flowing and calm. We have given you so much tonight.

We're going to close shortly, and Harry and I would like to thank you so much. Absorb these energies, be with them for a while; you will find as the days go by you will be much stronger.

We will leave you in Love and blessings; I will speak to you soon.

Anne added this immediately after the session:

So prior to starting the channelling with Diana I went upstairs and sat down quietly and said a prayer and opened to Spirit. Immediately Harry Edwards appeared to my right hand side and Diana to my left. All of a sudden the energies in my hands just started to change. I could feel energy coming in, coming into my whole body.

Now this isn't the first time that Diana and Harry Edwards have been with me. When we were in Poole (Dorset) a few weeks ago a young girl, who was only about 15 and was on the Healing Code workshop, who was quite psychic, came up to me and said she had seen Harry Edwards standing beside me, and also a lady in blue. She didn't know at that time that Harry Edwards was my Spirit guide, but I knew instantly that the lady was Diana.

Diana is making herself more to be seen, when we do these workshops. Two weeks ago on the Liverpool workshop, someone saw Diana at the side of me and also a nun. We don't know who the nun-is yet, it could have been mother Teresa, but we don't know that, and I haven't had any confirmation of that. So we will just have to see if this nun appears again.

I couldn't get the words out before [when the channelling began]; the words were all jumbled in my head.

CHAPTER TEN

APRIL 26TH

Well good afternoon, great to be back. It seems so long since I was here with you.

I want to move more on to healing, healing of the body, and how the body functions. I have said this book will not be a big book, it will only be a small book. There will be another book after this one, but I want to initially get the message out as fast as we can into this book.

So, let us talk about the body, your body, your magnificent body. There is a lot of talk going on at the moment about genes, about DNA, and 'junk' DNA.[32]

No.

The only junk in your body is what you consume. Either in food, drink, alcohol or drugs. Do you think that the Divine would make a body with junk in it? Absolute nonsense!

I'm speaking now of the 'junk' DNA. Yes, there are more strands of the DNA and they can be easily activated. And when these are activated it will give you immense knowledge and power. And you will be able to link in and see things more into the Spirit and psychic world.

Do you wonder why this DNA has been called 'junk'?

You need to be able to look into the body, and talk to the body.

God would never have made a body that was not perfect. You are perfect in every way; the imperfections come from within yourself. Everything that has been made by the Creator is perfect and works in absolute order. As you know, each cell talks to each other. What goes on in your body is more than a miracle. Far beyond miracles.

You take it and feed it with junk and wonder why it stops working. Open your eyes and see, your body is magnificent. It is an energy body, and when your energies get depleted, you then become tired. Energy depletion comes when you are stressed, when you are not feeling well.

There are ways you can stop that, and there are ways to improve the energy flow within the body. And everything we are talking about here is no big deal; it is very, very simple.

But there is a discipline.

And what we see up here is [that there is] hardly any discipline in your lives. You are quite happy to let other people run your lives for you. To run your health system for you, to run your body for you, to run your mind for you. Popping pills, medicines and goodness knows what.

But if we take the body as perfect, then what could go wrong? Really very little. The body was made to work, and as we have said before it wasn't made for illness. It was meant for wellness.

Looking after the body is paramount. The breathing is paramount. And the food intake. The body is highly intelligent, and will communicate with you. As you know, if you have an ache or a pain, and the ache or pain carries on you will know that something is not quite right. You can help by going into the body, speaking with the body and having a dialogue with it. And you will be very surprised with what you get back. And what you will get back will be the truth.

The body will tell you. Ask the body, what does it want? How can you help it? Even ask the body what food it wants. I will tell you without doubt that you will get the answers.

And of course we all know about thoughts, and at the moment we know that negative thoughts are intruding on your planet like never before. And that again is not just your thoughts out there, it is the collective consciousness of negative thoughts for so long. Which is almost destroying the Earth.

It affects the Earth's polarity. It affects your weather.[33] And people will laugh and say 'Don't be so ridiculous, how can thoughts do that?' But I can assure you thoughts are so powerful, because what you think then becomes an action. And if we get, as we have now anyway, deep dark negative thoughts it will upset the weather, it will upset the Earth, it will go into Mother Earth, as we spoke about before, and it pollutes everything.

We pollute each other, we pollute the ground we walk on, the air we breathe. So, we need to look, listen and take care of ourselves.

Now I have spoken before about meditation. I want to emphasise this again.

When we sleep our body is in healing mode. When we get into deep, deep sleep the body can heal and recover. And also it is energised. But many of you are still waking up feeling tired. Still feeling exhausted, as though you haven't slept. And I might add that sleep patterns are being interrupted as well. Because there are different energies, and they are having an effect on you, and we have spoken about this before in earlier chapters.

So, what does meditation do?

So as we align to the Creator we align to the cosmic energy so that cosmic energy can come into our body. It comes through the crown on the top of the head and goes through into the body. And in the body, in the cosmic energy lines – these are like branches, like little roots and these are all through the body – as these branches and filters are filled with cosmic energy then new life force comes into you.

It is imperative that you take some time, even if it is only 10 minutes a day, to be in silence, to be one with your Creator. To connect with the cosmic energy and bring that into your body.

You see, the ancients knew that this was a very, very powerful tool. When you are doing meditation it is from the heart. Our spark of the Divine Creator is in our heart too. So when we are meditating, and going into the heart, quietening the mind, then we are aligning with the one all mighty power. As we do this, the meditation has wonderful effects on the body. But in particular the heart.

And we know here that there are so many people suffering from heart problems.[34] Hardening of the heart. And do you wonder why?

Because people are hard. They take on all the gloom of the day, all the rubbish from the planets[35] and they can't see any further and their hearts harden to protect them. Or so they think. But this isn't protecting them; this in turn will cause problems. We were never meant to harden our hearts towards each other, we were meant to Love each other. This is why I say the only healer is Love.

That is why you are having all the heart attacks and all problems because you are not opening yourself up to the one true Love. The one true unconditional Love, your Creator. You are disconnecting and working with the material things in your life. And there is no satisfaction, no Love in that and it becomes greed, it becomes dog eat dog and it becomes competitive. And unless it stops, your heart issues will continue. It cannot go on as it is, with people trying to outdo each other.

What for?

We are here to take care of each other, old and young, black, yellow, white. It doesn't matter what colour the skin is, or what creed that people are. It matters that they are human beings, made with the Love and light of God.

And we should remember that.

Never judge anyone by the colour of their skin, or by their religion, or by the way they look. You are not here to judge, God doesn't judge. You are all equal in his eyes.

And the sooner you drop the veil from your eyes and see what's going on, the better everything will be.

So meditation again will soften the heart because you are going back to your source, back to your Creator. And just a few minutes a day [will give] enormous health benefits. It will help the blood to circulate better, it will help the lymphatic system to cleanse and move out all the toxins that accumulate in your body. It will help the liver, again to detoxify. And the kidneys. Everything in meditation is slowed right down. The main thing is that we become as near as we can to thought-lessness, to quieten our minds. And I know that is very difficult in this current age because you are bombarded 24/7 with your television, radio and the media. Everywhere you look. Your [advertising] hoardings as you walk down the street, everywhere you look you are bombarded with things to buy. It is so much more so than when I was here on your Earth plane, and I thought that was a shambles then. My goodness how much things have moved on and not for the better for humanity, not at all. Maybe for the profiteers but not for you.

So, slow the breathing down, slow the body down, slow the thinking down. You there [who] have bad circulation and have difficulty in walking, how different this would be if you could just spend 10 minutes or longer. 10 minutes just to help your own health.

You really need to wake up and do that! Take responsibility. It is far better than taking medication that is poisoning you.

We have talked before about organic food, pure water. The body is not meant to wear out as quickly as it is doing. Cells are renewed, so why should the body age and grow old the way you are doing at early ages?

You say now that you are living until your eightiess and nineties, but hundreds of years ago people would live well, well beyond that. In the Essene world people would live to beyond 140. And why was that? Because of their thoughts, their care of the mind and their care of the body. They cared for each other.

You are told that when you get to a certain age you will have this complaint and that complaint and you won't be able to do this and you won't be able to do that. And what are you doing at your age, and it is all down to age. That is total rubbish.

As I have said before, the body is a magnificent powerhouse. At the moment there are changes, and people are feeling it. But they are changes for the better; to align your body with changes that are coming in the next 2 to 3 years. In the next 2 to 3 months in fact.

You cannot stay stuck in this mire as you have been for these past 200 to 300 years.

There are so many different ways you can help your own healing. There are alternative ways. By aligning with your own chakra systems.[36] And using beautiful crystals.[37] Crystals are so powerful.

And a lot of these ways you can do yourself. You can read about them, try them out, and be open to new ideas. Well, new ideas I say, but these ideas have been around a lot, lot longer than you or I.

We have lost the path; we need to get back onto the path, to get back to the way we used to heal. You have it in the palm of your hands to help yourself heal. More so than you ever know, and you ever think.

You have to take responsibility and only you can do it. It may be strange to those of you who have never had healing or understood it, but there is nothing mystical or magical about it. It is the most natural thing. We were brought into creation to be able to heal each other and to heal ourselves.

Be aligned with your body. Walk. I don't suggest you do massive exercise, I don't feel that's good for you. In the long-term, and in many ways, it can be harmful. Pounding and pounding your feet and your legs, if it is kept up it doesn't do them any good. But gentle exercise. Walking, yoga, tai chi, the ancient arts. That is what you should be looking at. To rediscover the Chi, life force energy. Bring that into your body. As I have said, there are number of things there to bring the cosmic energy into your body. And in that way you will find there will be no illness because, as the cosmic energy comes into your body, any areas that are depleted will be re-aligned and replenished with cosmic energy from God. That is how it has always been, always should have been.

We have been told different, we have not been told the truth. Now you know how to do it. We look down and see you here from Spirit, and we see what you are doing to yourselves and it makes our hearts so sad. Even if you just do it step-by-step, look at your diet, cut out the fats, please cut out the fizzy drinks.

Knowing that if you are putting junk into your body, that is what you will be, junk.

Unable to be fit, unable to think clearly, unable to feel good. And, as I have said before, God never made you with anything in your body that is not used. The DNA that is being called 'junk' DNA will be, and can be, brought back to life.

And this will start happening to people now. Well it is already happening and it will make an incredible difference to all that you see, opening you up psychically, giving you an inner strength, an inner knowledge that has been lying dormant for so long. Just note that things are changing and changing fast and neither you [n]or I can stop them. Nor would I want to. It is for the best for all of you.

Jack, I think you had some questions?

Thank you again Diana for this priceless wisdom. I always laugh when I formulate questions prior to the channelling and then you answer most of them as you speak. But there are a couple I want to ask you and one is what you've just been talking about, the magnificence and the beauty of the body. How is it when certain children are born with deformities or all of us are poisoned by what's going on in the world, the fluoridation of water, the chemtrails in the air and so on.[38] *These changes of cosmic energy can they overcome these issues?*

Of course. Cosmic energy is from God and you know also that the power of prayer can change so much. We're not on about children now of course but pollution, chemtrails. If people would just open their eyes and just reconnect themselves with the world of Spirit, the world of God, whatever they want to call it then so much could be done and it can be done so quickly.

We know there are people poisoning the planet, we are aware of that, but I would suggest that when you see the chemtrails just pray. For although the chemtrails will stay there, praying will remove the toxicity. And I would always suggest, and I know Anne does this anyway, just hold your hands over your food and pray silently. And I know you will taste the difference in your food and your drinks and your water. And you know about the messages from water, and all you have to do is label your water with the words 'Love' on it and that vibration will change that water that you drink. You don't have to go and buy expensive bottled water. Just write on the bottles.

You see, everybody wants to make things so complicated and really they are not. God never made anything complicated. You, humans, have made everything complicated. When you strip it all back to the bone, really human life isn't and shouldn't be complicated.

You asked about children Jack, could you just ask me that again?

We often see kids on the television who have so-called incurable diseases, or kids who were born with deformities for whatever reason. Although I'm 100% behind what you just said I'm wondering, is there any other way we can overcome these things?

There are a number of ways and that is a very big question. There are three areas there. Sometimes children are born with deformities, and I know some people might find this hard, we choose when we come back into this world and if we have lessons to learn we may choose to come back maybe as a child like that. Or choose to be within a particular family, a soul group. When we reincarnate and when we go back to Spirit we go within what is known as our soul group. So you know when you meet people, you know, you feel as if you have known then before. This is because they are part of your soul group. You will encounter these people lifetime after lifetime in different forms, in different people. They may be male, they may be female. We always stay within the same soul group. Some of these children will come back to be within that soul group. Maybe to be cared for and to be loved. And some will come back just for a short time for that experience of coming into human form. And then they will go back to Spirit.

Some of the illnesses that children are having today can be eradicated. I know that there is a great big blown up [case] of children having asthma. And that is again being caused through stress. A lot is through diet, fizzy drinks, fats, and lots of carbohydrates. The body needs some but not like we are seeing today. Sugar, absolutely sugar, and all the things that follow on from sugar.

In ancient times we didn't have sugar, we had honey. But now they are having the saccharine, the one calorie sweeteners,[39] which we know are full of chemicals. But all these chemicals are put into the fizzy drinks and that affects the children. That is why you get children being naughty and being disobedient because they are hyperactive with the caffeine that is put in, and the chemicals that are put into the drinks.

The food people are very, very canny. We talked about this with your friends yesterday. They will label [them] vitamin drinks, healthy drinks and goodness–knows-what drinks. And to the mother who wants to do the best for their children and thinks they are will buy them blindly.

It is all about educating people as to what additives are going into food. [Certain] metals are toxic as we know so children with all kinds of ailments [should have] their diets looked into, and their stresses looked into.

Because people think children don't have stresses! But of course they do. Most of the stresses start in childhood, carry on, and then erupt later in life. They are still there and start within childhood, as you know in the work that you do some of them start with the foetus.

That is when all the problems do start, in the growing of the baby, and the birthing. Total separation. That is why years ago, when mothers had children at home, that was much, much better. And I know now it is coming back and I welcome that. Where babies can be born at home, where there is no risk why shouldn't they? Why do they have to be hospitalised and the babies taken away?

Everything needs to go back to nature, to basics. That doesn't mean to say we go back to the dark ages, of course not. But with the care of the doctors and the midwives a home birth is perfect. Look how many animals give birth without anybody being there.

So we need to look at these things now. We have just galloped so far ahead in the last 40 years I would say a lot of things have happened with people because they thought it was the right way to do it, thinking that this is the way forward, but the way has been lost.

Caring has been lost and it just becomes a [machine] factory in some of the hospitals giving birth when it should be quite precious. Because that is quite an ordeal when that child comes into the world. Not, maybe, for the first time as a soul but as that human child for the first time. And just the separation from the mother's womb into the bright lights is quite a shock for that small, tiny little baby. That baby has everything it needs within it. God has made sure of that, but of course it does want to be nurtured, it does want to be fed, and be cleaned. That baby will thrive with the nurturing and the food and it has built into it its own immune system.

Does that answer your question Jack?

It does, but there are others. I suppose a follow-on question would be, given the damage that has been caused in the way you described, and if we could put right the diet, is it possible the healing that you are channelling through Anne, and will share with us, could solve some of these problems and rectify even some pretty severe cases?

It does depend on the cases. As you know, you work with cellular memory; it is not quite so clear cut. I would like to have said of course, and yes in many ways it will, but again you have to consider other things that have gone on in previous lifetimes, if you look into that, and maybe karma. I don't wish to discuss [karma] at this point – there are many, many books on karma – but I think in the majority of cases we will have some profound healings. And I will say, in most cases, there will be healing.

But again, as you know, what happens is not in our hands. It is in the hands of God. We can only do God's work and give 150% as I know you and others on the Earth plane are now doing. We appreciate that so much here in Spirit. We see what you are doing, we see how it wears you out, we see that sometimes it isn't an easy task, but a very rewarding and fulfilling task. Without people like yourselves, this world, this planet – and let me make this very clear – would have no chance of surviving. But there are so many now, so many working in different fields. Not just healing; telling the truth of what's going on. Opening up these old chests, treasure chests, that have been locked up for so long – but they haven't got treasure in them – and when the truth is out we can work with that, and healing will come from that also.

I know sometimes it may seem like just travelling on and on and on but there are people opening up now. For every seminar you do now, most of those people will open up. Because they come because they want to. And there are other people doing work – and I know you have other friends such as Brett,[40] and people you were with yesterday, doing the Deeksha,[41] and all this energy is accumulating as a powerful positive energy.

The more people who do it, as I have said time and time again, [the more] the positive energy will just absorb the negativity. So it is a never ending journey. A never, never ending journey. And I'm so pleased I am here and I can help you. I do travel around quite a bit and connect sometimes with Judith, Anne's friend, to tell Judith I am connecting with Anne and to give her messages that she passes on.

Sometimes it is a very different space you are in when you are doing this work. But we know we have people channelling Jesus and channelling Mary all over the world now, and channelling other Masters as well. Jay Atkinson[42] with Solomon. And it is growing and growing. And you know we are so pleased here, so pleased that all the people you are connecting with, it's all meant to be.

If I can say, cast your nets wider. We need that here in Spirit. We will help you all we can. Cast the nets as wide and as far as you can. To spread all this wonderful work that you are doing. Is there anything else Jack?

Thank you again Diana. Yes just one last question. Self-evidently, you came to Anne. I can only speak for myself, because you are coming through Anne, I am eternally grateful. But is it possible, because I know you and her were together as Essenes, is it possible in her subconscious that she invited you in, in this lifetime?

I chose to come in to Anne.[43] So I would say on this occasion, no. I made the decision, I made the choice. Because of the qualities I needed to get this message out, and the people we need to get this out to. I wanted it to be pure of heart and understandable to everyone who even doesn't understand spiritual things. I want this to open up people to the Spirit side of life. Not just to Diana. If we can open people up to this through the workshops and through the book, and through talks and anything else then we are doing a most fabulous, wonderful job. Is there anything else you want to ask about that?

No, just to thank you once again. Like you, I have missed these sessions and look forward to the next one.

Now, as I have said, this is not going to be a huge book. I think now we are possibly 50 to 60% through this book. And I would say there is stuff that needs to be looked at now to explain things that you need to be looking at. I know there was channelling that Anne did earlier in the year when I had her up at ridiculous hours. And I apologise for that, but I needed to get through with the messages. They will be at the beginning of the book. It needs to be looked at, and you need to get it into chapters and you need to bring in more stuff. As you read through it you will know what to do.

Anne has got the symbol, and we did have a conversation earlier in the therapy room about the symbol. I want the colours of the symbol to be very, very dark blue. Very deep, crystal-type blue. She knows in her mind... and then lighter shades of blue into it. I have given her the colours in her mind.

I will leave you now and we will come back much sooner than the last time. Thank you.

MAY 7TH

So welcome, and thank you for inviting me back today. There are so many changes in your world and over the last week I have noticed so many changes again.

So many lies in your newspapers. So many lies again about me.[44] I have noticed that is coming up to the front again. I will just say do not believe all you see, hear and read.

However, today I want to talk about the mind. The mind can be a wonderful tool but can also take us into the realms of darkness and despair. We need our mind to help us go through the day and [for] our daily routine. Our mind can give us wonderful inspiration and thoughts, but most of these inspirations and thoughts come from the Universe and from God.

We have to keep the mind open. A lot of illnesses, mental illnesses and anxieties are caused because the mind is closed. The mind has a thought that works upon another thought, that works upon another thought and, before we know [it], we have a monster. A monster of thoughts we have created within our heads. I know because I did this many years ago when I was on the Earth plane. The slightest thing would get me into the darkest of moods; until those thoughts and those moods would get me to be suicidal.

And you think that there is no way out as I did. You go further and further down the slippery road. The road of no return.

So it is about taking control of our mind. People say 'Well that's easy to do', well yes it is for most people, but when you are in the state that I was in, it was incomprehensible to even think of taking control of my mind. My mind was controlling me. Days and nights and months it went on. I was totally out of control with my thoughts, with my actions, with my deeds. With what I said and what I did.

But after, when I was in the Spirit world and had control, when [on Earth] I had worked through it, it is easy to come out of it but you do need help. It may only be one kind word that can snap you out of it. Or it may take a little bit more.

At this moment in time, it is all about the powers that be making us fearful, making us scared and frightened. And I know some people are even in terror about what is going on in the world, just what is going on in your world. And when we are in this terror, when we are in this fear, then it is easy to control us. Because one fear knocks on to another fear and we read in the newspapers, or we catch the news with another fear.

Whatever flu it is going to be, whatever shortage it is going to be; whatever, whatever, whatever it is going to be will put you in horrendous torment. Shortage of money, shortage of jobs, mortgage hikes, fuel hikes, you name it they have got it all there and all mapped out for you.

But once you can see, once you can know and once you can drop into your heart you will find answers there very different [to those] that are in your head. Truthful answers.

The mind will play games with you and make [up] stories. It will gather false information that you will believe is real, but it isn't. Most of the time it is false and it is this that sends you into the spiral of darkness.

Dropping into the heart, asking the heart, asking the Universe, asking God to help you, to give you answers... The heart will give you the right answers.[45]

People will say 'How do I do that? It is difficult.' And we know it isn't, because you [Anne and Jack] have done it. But when people are in despair they cannot think and realise that just a small change, just a small switch, of dropping into the heart sometimes is all that is needed. And it is that simple. Maybe you could imagine a small switch? Or a dial. Anything that will take you from your head into your heart.

While we are in the mindset of terror and fear it is having an effect on our body, on our breathing, on our heart, lungs, on every organ of the body. And of course, as we know, this is what causes a high percentage of your illnesses.

So we need to be kind to the mind. Sometimes, when we are given thoughts, ask the mind, 'Are these my thoughts?' We are in negative centres – in the UK and all over the world – and there are more parts of the world that are negative. We are surrounded by an ocean of negativity. Sometimes we can tap into other people's thoughts.

Ask the mind, 'Are these really my thoughts?' And although that might sound strange, wait for the answer. If it is 'yes' then welcome them and give thanks. And if it is 'no' ask for them to be sent back with Love and blessings to their original owner. You don't need to know who that is – the Universe will know and will do that for you.

You need to tame the mind; we need to control it with kindness and with Love. Thoughts that come in, let them pass. And if they won't pass, just send Love to them, and maybe ask what are they doing for you? Sometimes the mind has your best interests at heart, although it may not seem so when all these black, doubting thoughts come in.

Stop a while, and ask the mind 'Why have you given me this thought, what am I to do with it?' Breathe into the thought; breathe Love into the thought; kindness, compassion. And, as you breathe that into the thought, see how the thought changes. See what colour the thought changes to and before long, having done this, you will notice the thought that may have looked very dark will be infused with the Love and light of God. And that thought will become light. And will disappear.

Don't let the mind take complete control of you. This may take a little while, and you may have to do this a few times a day, but be aware of what [thoughts are] coming in and stop them. And if need be, be quite firm; you don't want these thoughts. And ask them to go away, send them back to whom they came from. Send them back to God to be infused with Love and light.

As you do this, little by little, step-by-step your mind will become clear and you will find that you will have a smile, and you may even have a gladness in your heart.

And we work through this, and with the body, and with the food I have spoken about previously and with pure clear water, watching the intakes of any chemicals. Slowly, slowly you will be able to come to lighter, fresher thoughts.

Start every day with a prayer, be it however small. Set your intention with the prayer to fulfil your day with Love and kindness. Ask God for whatever you need that day, God will never refuse. Ask for kindness, ask for Love, and ask for money. Whatever you ask for will come. It may not be in that instance but it will come to you. God never refuses. And, as you heal your mind, your body will also heal and grow stronger.

You are not meant to dwell in darkness. This [the darkness] has been [created] purposely and this has been done by feeding the mainstream media with so much darkness and gloom and terror that it is almost unspeakable what the media and the powers that be are trying to do to the population.

There is enough for everyone on this planet, God makes sure of that. But you are told the opposite. Even though the planet is a little overcrowded, there is enough for everyone if the greedy ones would just but share.

I want you to go through your day with Love and appreciation for all that you have knowing, that if you give Love and gratitude, whatever you have will grow. Know that always God gives you what you need for that day. And so we do that the following day and the same thing happens.

Although the people on the planet [the current rulers] have power there is no greater power than universal Love and God. There is no greater power. But when we become disconnected from our God this is when we lose our power. This is when we start to doubt. This is when things start to go a little awry. This is when things seem to be muddled.

Once you start again to connect with your source, to your giver of life, things will start to go on the right path for you. Know that, within your heart, you carry the spark or the seed of your Creator. And so you are the Creator. All of you are Creators and don't forget that. Don't let the darkness overshadow you and overcrowd you. And, even if you are at their lowest ebb, pop your head above the parapet. Look around, and little by little get your strength to come out and walk in the sunshine. You are a child of God. All of you. Your life is meant to be full of sunshine and light.

But, over so many thousands of years, the human race has been manipulated and now it is time to bring your power back. To connect to your source, to bring the power back into your heart, and to be at one with yourself and with God.

And to share, and to be kind to all your friends and all the people you meet on your path. And, as you spread the kindness and happiness and Love, they will see it in your face and in your eyes, and they will think 'there is something in this, I want to feel better, I want some of that Love and kindness.' And knowing that as you give it out you will get it back, and you will get it back tenfold.

Keep your thoughts kind and pure, be pure of heart. I don't mean when we say that here in Spirit, to be 'pure' and never to have a drink or fun. Pure of heart means something different; it means caring for your fellow beings. Your animals, every creature on the planet. Because in every creature, in everything that lives and breathes, is part of everyone. We are part of everything, the trees and the plants, as I have spoken of many times before.

We are all linked to each other, be it human, animal or vegetable matter. We are all linked, and we all need each other. And when you all realise that, by harming each other, by harming an animal or harming the trees, [you are harming yourself] how much better your planet will be. God created everything to work in harmony with each other and man has broken that harmony. So much to the degree now that you are in danger, but we are working here and we know there are many, many light workers now. And, as you spread this out, of course the light workers will grow and the planet will become filled with light instead of darkness.

And we all, certainly here in Spirit, can rest a little and you can all live in peace and Love. Not in fear and terror. The fear and terror is man-made to keep you down, to stop you from knowing and reaching your full potential. We want you to be at one with each other. I want you to send Love out even if you just sit quietly at home or in your office. Just send, from your heart, Love to people you may not even know. But know, as you send this Love out to all four corners of the Earth, it will be felt and make a vast difference to every living creature.

Sit quietly, play beautiful music and send that Love out from your heart and give thanks to the Universe and to God for all that you have and all that you can give to others just by sending that Love vibration out.

As you send that Love vibration out, as you sit in circles around your planet or alone. Send that Love vibration out. If you could see what changes it is making it would lift your hearts so much you would never want to stop doing it.

We see that here in Spirit, we see the difference it makes, the energy that changes in your world. And it is so wonderful, so, so wonderful. And as you spread this word and spread this Love – and I know you talk of a critical mass – [as] more people that do this, we can tip the points of this planet and we can change the world. Then you will live in peace and harmony, far more than you are now

But you have to do it. Only the human race can do it. We are here helping and guiding, but you yourselves must do this work.

Slowly and gently, as each person realises what they can give to each other, and what they can give to the whole planet then life will change. And it can change in the twinkling of an eye.

I beg you to spread this word and send Love. For that's all we have and all we are. Pure God-given Love.

I'm going to close there now unless you have any questions Jack?

Yes Diana, I do have a couple, and thank you again for the wonderful wisdom. You mentioned the Earth being overcrowded.

I have read plans about the people who are running the planet to kill most of us so that the population goes down to around 500 million.[46] *I'm wondering what your observations on that are?*

Well, they will try of course but the more of you who can shed light on this, the better. A lot of these people have come down – however ridiculous it may sound to you – people have come down to help the planet, to lighten the planet. Yes some will go, some will go of their own accord. Because when they find out, as I have said previously, when they find out what has gone on they will not be able to comprehend, and take in, and understand...and they will leave this planet.

I'm sure you will notice there are people leaving the Earth plane now. Some of them are quite young, but they have done their work here you see. When people have done their work, they will leave.

They ['the powers that be'] will try, and they have already done it in the past. We know that. And they will try again. And some people will pass. But the more people who know what is happening – and wow how this is spreading and how pleased we are – the more people know what is going on, the more people will be able to save the planet.

But I do have to say, some people will leave of their own accord and some people will leave because of what is happening to your food, and this is why I say please be careful about the food you eat.

I would say this, and I know that Anne does it sometimes, please get the message out of blessing the food. If you bless the food, then God, the Universe and source can take away the contamination. It is simple. And if you can pass this on to the people you work with and talk to, to bless the food, that blessing is so powerful and it will take away the contamination, and chemicals, and the negativity of thoughts. While this food is coming from all over the world, of course, it is picking up the fears and the negativity and whatever else is happening on the planet.

So, by blessing the food, you will release toxins, negativity, chemicals and you will balance the food and you will notice it will taste better. Try it. Taste the food before you bless it, bless it and I tell you – and Anne knows this because she does it, not all the time but a lot of times she does it with the wine – blessing will take out the toxins and purify your food, your wine, your drink. Is that OK?

Thank you. And I suspect every time you come, and I anticipate a question you cover it! One thing has been going through my mind for the last few days. The healing that we spread using the Healing Code – and we will be using your material – works very quickly and we know this causes some people problems because it appears to be too quick. But one thing that has been going through my mind is that some people need a bit longer; need us to stay with them for longer. I'm wondering if you have any views on that, and how we perhaps might do it, because this is something that would help us as well. Rather than just do this with one or two sessions, and all your wisdom through this book will help – and that is why I was laughing before because you are offering a prescription for life – is there something missing?

For example, if someone has a chronic illness and we do a couple of sessions, perhaps they need a bit more and I'm wondering what your observations are on that?

There is nothing missing.

Let me tell you there is nothing missing.

I didn't think there was!

Yes some people need more. We know of the quick fixes. I've been there, you've been there. Let me tell you I've been there. Of course the person themself has to want to heal, we all know that. You see, there are times when I didn't want to heal and I didn't heal. There are times I didn't heal because of what was going on; yes it was a cry for help. But if people want to heal, as you know, you are almost there.

But I would say now you look at a programme, maybe a 4 to 6 session programme doing the Healing Code but also bringing in other things that will come into your mind. I want you to bring into these programmes some information on nutrition for them; foods they eat. Because of what's gone on in people's lives you never know how long it is going to take. You know as you are doing the Healing Code they are becoming more and more powerful, but some people may want a number of sessions.

What I have in my mind is you work for some people for 4 to 6 sessions including talking about the nutrition and breathing and their lifestyle.

I don't ever see you becoming a crutch for people; the Healing Code is fast and it works well. Sometimes, if people have been through so much, they do need a crutch for a while. I did. And they need people they can trust and I know what I'm talking about, because I was so lonely and I felt I had no one who I could trust. So don't be concerned about people coming to see you more than once or twice. After all, if people had these conditions for many years, maybe a life-time, what if they come to you for a dozen sessions?

Don't be concerned. Some people will be helped so much by having those extra sessions.

I do think, over the next few months or so, you will bring more about lifestyles and well-being into the programme you're going to be using. And it can all be kept very simple. The simpler and easier for people the better, because they are so bombarded with [complexity] everywhere you look today; they need simple remedies, simple healings. Simple Love. Simple food. You have the knowledge to do this. And other ideas will come to you over the next few days and weeks.

I don't feel you will be able to cram all this into one day so you may have to look at, in some cases, 1½ to 2 days.

Sometimes, because people are so bombarded, they are coming for one-to-ones and to the workshops with so much in their heads, it is not always going in as it should and sometimes they need a little bit of extra help. Maybe re-fresher courses. That is for you to decide.

You are doing a wonderful job and you know the people that you help. And we see it here and we are very grateful for it. OK?

Thank you Diana.

Is there anything else?

There always is, but by the time you next visit us you will have come with the answers!

I do listen in you know, I am aware of what's going on.

What we want here in Spirit is to get people reconnected to God. To have a better life than they are having now. Because it saddens us so much to see people in so much distress and with so much hurt in their hearts and it needn't be. But we understand the pressures that you are under, pressures from governments, pressure from everywhere. Everywhere you turn there is a pressure or a threat, but just remember there is no person, no one person, not even groups of people who are more powerful than your one God.

And keep that in mind.

God will never let you down. Many people can reconnect, you know this is what happens. They reconnect, hooking back up to God, the Universe, then things become clearer and you can work through things that are coming at you at one hundred – well a thousand miles an hour – I would say. But it is when people become unhooked they lose it mentally and physically. The world looks a shambles. We see it here in the Spirit world and we are orchestrating the moves that need to be made.

While it may look a shambles to people on the planet, we are sorting it out. And with the likes of the light workers like yourself and Anne. Although you know we need more, we are [getting] there step-by-step. And quicker than we thought, and so we need to make this quicker and easier for everyone. Does that answer your question?

Absolutely. Again, thank you.

So I leave you now with Love and light, not just from me but from all the people and the guardians here in our world of Spirit and Love. And until we meet again.

[Anne: I can always tell when it's coming to an end because my eyes start to itch.]

CHAPTER TWELVE

MAY 21ˢᵀ

Well, welcome this evening.
It is a pleasure to be here.
And, of course, I have now
met Jimmy![47] So, good evening Jimmy.

It makes my heart smile to
look at him; he is such a
beautiful creature, and a very

intelligent cat. And it is no coincidence that he is here with
us tonight because we are going to talk about the heart, and
Love and gratitude. And what gives you more Love and
gratitude than an animal?

There are no coincidences; Jimmy knew and wanted to be
in on this.

So we have talked about the heart now many times. But it
is so important. And I think you know, the more work you
do, the more people you meet and see, that only the heart
and Love can work on this planet.

We are so pleased to have so many light workers, and
every day the numbers are growing and you are all doing such
wonderful work. And we are on our way.

The sky and the Heavens are filled with Love for you all
here. We know it has been difficult in the last few weeks with
all the planetary changes. We know that some of you have felt
very unwell and very low. But we have to align your bodies as

the energy on the planet is lightening. And the dark, deep energies that have been around for so long are crumbling away.

Finer energies are now coming in and you will all feel a little bit better and a little bit more upbeat. There is now an opening of the heart chakra and each one of you is being touched with this. And, of course, some of your hearts are already open. And that's wonderful and we really appreciate that, because when the heart is open it can give and receive so much Love.

Some of your hearts are only just opening. And that's also wonderful because it will be a wonderful experience for you. An experience to see into another being. To be that other being, to feel what that other being is feeling. And also it will make you understand not to criticise people, not to judge, because in judging them we are but judging ourselves.

Everyone has a hurt that needs healing; some more than others. So do not judge others when they look down or miserable because it will be the bearing of a hurt, maybe a long time buried hurt. We will never know as we pass that person in the street.

Just send Love to them.

Do not think this is just a word. Feel that Love as you pass that person; send it from your heart. And I will tell you this. That person will know, and that person will feel better. And that will help to open their hearts as well. And we can come back to where we used to be; loving and heart centred. Like our animals, like Jimmy.

Like the deer in the forest caring for each other. You have no idea how your world will change. You have absolutely no idea. With the loving and the sharing of each heart, how this world will transform. It will be not short of Paradise because everything grows on Love. You know if you give Love to a flower or a plant that will grow. And if you nourish it and nurture it with tenderness you will see the beauty in the plant. And we are all like plants; we all want to be loved and to be touched, and to be admired. Not in an egotistical way but to be admired for the beauty and Love that shines forth from us.

Do not judge others. As I have said, we never know how deep they are hurting. And by judging others we are judging ourselves. And that doesn't help us in any way. It has a negative effect on our bodies and our cells and the organs of the body. We have been born into negativity, we have been programmed into negativity, and it is now [time] to change.

While we are negative we can be used, while we are in fear. But when we change, when we change our hearts and go with Love, then the fear drops away and you find your real true self. The you that has always been, but has been programmed. But we can strip all that away. And it is being stripped away; we do this slowly. But in the last few months we have increased the vibrations because we want to accelerate the healing.

So easy is it to Love another person, or an animal or a tree or a plant. We are all vibrating, everything vibrates at energy level. And if you were to go and be fearsome to a tree that tree would feel that vibration. But if you were to hold that tree, and Love that tree, again it would feel that loving energy. For everything that you touch with Love, humans, animals, trees, everything that you touch with Love, they vibrate Love out.

So it isn't just about loving each other and changing the world; it is [about] loving everything *to* change the world. Even the little seedlings in the ground. The frogs in the pond. The birds. Even down to the blades of grass in your lawn or in your gardens. We are all living, vibrating energies. And we are all connected. The soil and the Earth that you walk on, right up to the stars in the sky. We are all connected, all vibrating. And the more we can all vibrate the Love vibration, wow, it will be incredible.

Change your thoughts about your neighbours and your friends. If they irritate you, know that they are not doing it to you, they are doing it unthinkingly. Just send them the vibration of Love. There is not a living thing on the planet that does not want, and will accept, Love. It is the only thing. It heals, has power, helps growth in your fields and in your crops. And you already know any food that is cooked with Love tastes so much different to anything that is put together without a thought. Love the food that you cook. Know that it is given to you with Love from the Creator, from God.

That brings me on to gratitude. Gratitude is very, very powerful. To say thank you for all the things in your life that we take for granted. The more we thank God, the Creator for all the things you have in your life then the Creator knows you like what you are getting. And the Creator only wants to please you; you are his children. He does not want to harm you in any way; He wants you to have the best. That's how it was in the beginning; all his children had the best. The Love, the food, they didn't have any shortage.

So as you give gratitude for everything that you have then your supply will multiply. But just giving gratitude isn't enough; you have to feel it from your heart. Not just say it as a passing remark. It has to be felt deep, deep within the heart. Even for the very smallest things. The water that you have, and your food. The soap that you wash yourself with, and the petrol and the cars. Everything that is taken on an everyday basis for granted. Think how all these things got to you. Who brought them? Who worked to bring you the food that you got on your plate? The fuel for your car? The electricity to heat your home?

So give thanks to the Universe for all these wonderful things. You will be amazed at the turnaround in your life. Because, [when] God knows you are grateful and you are happy with what He is supplying then your supply will increase. Don't take my word for it, try it and see.

A simple thing from when you get up in the morning to when you go to bed at night. Just give thanks for all the little things and the big things that pass in your life each day.

Do you have any questions Jack?

I do Diana, and I would just like to say I'm getting withdrawal symptoms because it seems a long time since you were last here.

It has been a long time.

Through no one's fault of course.

No, you, Anne and myself have to get together when the time is right. But it is no coincidence and we make the time, the right time.

So, as we are getting towards the end of the book I have written to a number of publishers. Could we accelerate that in any way, I would be grateful for your advice?

Well I would certainly write again to Yellowfin publishers. And you may have to write to a number of smaller publishers, but it will happen, it will be published. We in Spirit here will make sure of that, and I think you will have 2 to 3 offers. Just let them know about it, they can't come to you unless they know. Send it out to the Universe, let the publishers know what you have and they will contact you. Does that make sense?

Totally, thanks. I think what was behind the question was, doubt isn't the right word, and I know it will be published, are all things that are going on at the moment. As you know we are grecophiles. It concerns me what is going on in Greece.[48] *Do you have any thoughts as how it is likely to play out?*

I think there is going to be a very sharp turnaround in favour of the Greek people. I cannot say how that will be, and there are a lot of things to be dealt with. I know you are [particularly] concerned about the youth, but things can't be done overnight. People on this planet, certain people as you know, have got us into this mess. We, I will help and the people have to help get themselves out of it. It is not going to be an overnight wonder, but I do think it will be quite amazing what will happen. The Greeks are very strong people and they will come through this, and they will come through this stronger and better and they will not be put on and walked on like they have been in the past. As I say, it cannot be done overnight but it will be put right over time.

Again, that is what I suspected. Another question, which is perhaps an interesting one. I was watching a film the other day about trans-humanism.[49] *A lot of people are being led down the path of technology being the solution to our current problems. To the extent of micro-chipping people, and having parts of themselves plugged into computers. This is an option that people who are running the planet are offering and I suspect a lot of people will fall for it. I would like your observations.*

Yes, some people will fall for it. And we can't stop them. I will tell you this. In the last 40 years or maybe a little longer, technology has gone at too fast a pace for humanity. People cannot cope with the quickness of how everything is going. Let me tell you, it is causing turmoil within the mind. And that is part of some of the problems. The mind problems, the anxieties that you are having today. It is not just the way people are living, as you say, in the fast lane but our brains were never made to take electronic information and electronic equipment into our minds as fast as they have over the last 40 years. And, as you know, it is still accelerating. It will, as we say with some people, blow their minds. It has already done with a number of people. The brain cannot cope because it is coming in too fast and too rapid[ly]. Although the human brain can cope with many things, and has a huge capacity, it is the information and how it is coming in that is the problem.

And that's because it affects the left brain[50] rather than the right brain.

Yes. And what is happening is that the two are tangling together and there is confusion in many, many people.

Of course this is deliberate.

Unfortunately, and sadly it is. People want to learn and become more technical; they think it is the be all and end all but you and I know it certainly isn't. There is only one thing, and it isn't the brain, and it isn't technology. You know it is Love and Love from the heart. And, until people get that and feel that, we are going to have these confusions and these anxieties. And you will notice the anxieties are getting far worse and in younger people too. There is so much pressure. We were never meant to absorb all this information so quickly. We were meant to change and to grow and to have the new technology but it is coming in too fast for most humans to cope.

Thank you. The last question is a personal question. It may seem trivial but I've been looking for ways in which to heal my eyes[51] with various modalities that we use so that I no longer need glasses. I seem to keep running into cul-de-sacs with this. Again it is a knowing that I can do it and it can be done. I'm almost loath to ask you, but do have any insights?

You can do it and it can be done. And you know better than I do but what about the question 'What don't you want to see?' You know that, but you know it can be done. You know more about the healing than many, many people but you have to ask yourself, do you truly want your eyes healed? And if you do, the question is answered. We feel here in Spirit that there is nothing that cannot be healed but sometimes it is that human's time to pass into our world [and] sometimes it isn't. And it is through stress, and through certain abuse of the body, that can cause stress and anxieties, that will accelerate them coming here to Spirit. There is so much healing; there is so much pain that can be healed if people would only take responsibility for their own lives instead of handing it over to others.

And we know not everybody is capable of doing this; some people are in [such] torment in their minds and hearts that they can't take this on by themselves.

But, as you know, the work you are doing, the energy work in whatever form that comes in is the healing of the future. And it will get quicker, not immediately because we here in Spirit know how much the human body can take, so shall we say drip feed out, because the body can only take certain amounts of energy. But it is accelerating as you are aware and the healing you are doing and others [are doing] in the energy field is just wonderful and can help so many people. We know, here in the Spirit world, that energy healing can touch people so quickly and make them healthy and well. And to give that health to someone who is really suffering – what is more precious than that? Because all the money cannot buy your health, cannot repair your body. And, as you know, the healing intelligence that you work with really is one of the main things to heal our bodies.

Yes, we need the medical profession, not in the way it is now; it has gone out of control with the medications. We need them for some operations as I have said before. We need them for accidents; they do wonderful, wonderful work. But some of their work could be taken care of if people would turn to energy healings and other healings, Reiki[52] – that is an energy healing of course – but looking after themselves is more preventative than letting things get a firm hold.

And even, as you know, when we start with a small pain it is a signal that our lives are too stressful. But, unfortunately, a lot of people don't know how to deal with it. They are so accustomed to going to the doctor, that's how they have been brought up for probably 50 years. But it is so ridiculous to get yourself so ill and then go and just pop a pill and expect to be okay. It isn't like that. You have to take care of the body, we also have to take care of the stress within the body and the mind. The mind can really get out of control and that is where a very good proportion of the stress, most of the stress, comes by thoughts. Critical thoughts, unhealthy thoughts about ourselves and others. And of course if we give unkind thoughts to other people it resonates within their bodies and their cells but also yours and ours as you are giving them out. And I have done this in my past. I've had bad thoughts about people, I've cursed and when I was in human form I know it has a boomerang effect. You do it when you're upset because it is the only way you know; hurting another person makes you feel better. Maybe for a short time. We all know that's not right and that has been human conditioning and that's what we want to try and change now with going into the heart centre.

If people are kind and closer to each other, and care for each other, again that will cut down a lot of your health problems.

If you could see when someone says angry words, if you could see the energy going from that person to the other person it is almost like knives going into the body. Knives of energy and that has an immense effect. And so, by saying either nothing or saying kind words, again that will turn your health system around.

There is so much you can all do and it is all really easy. Yes it is all right for you to say, Diana. You're sat there. Of course, but I've had and done a lot of these things, good and bad. I was no Angel some of the time when I was on the Earth. I know by changing thoughts and being kinder and caring for each other in any small way has such a vast, magnificent effect on not only the other person, not only you but on people surrounding you. If you are shouting and angry then that energy is coming from you and is extending out into your vibration. And, of course that will have an effect if there is anybody within that vibration – it will affect them. So, caring and sharing is a huge step for humans on the planet to change things.

Any more questions Jack?

No, just three short comments. Firstly there may only be a very short time before we can actually see the energy as you describe it like knives. Secondly, even though I never see you in the way that Anne does – maybe one day I will maybe I won't – I was very conscious of your presence on the Sunday. I feel it rather than see it.

Yes, my energy was with the group on Sunday and what a beautiful energy that was, absolutely high-energy and lifts us all here in Spirit. We see, and feel, and we can come among you and we just say here in Spirit world, spread this as I know you are and we are helping you. Spread this out now, we know you have worked so hard over the last almost 2 years without financial reward but that is going to change. So many people out there trust you and when they know you they have no doubt about any of the teachings you are giving them. Because they know it comes totally, totally from the centre of your heart. So it is just a matter of a little time, a little patience and things will start to grow very well for you.

We need people like you and, I've said this on a number of occasions, the more you can spread this whether it is the Diana workshops, the Healing Code workshops or whatever heart based workshop that you do then we are so grateful here. It is just lighting one candle isn't it, and a 1000 more will shine.

So, we thank you here in Spirit, thank you for your hard work. We are now connecting you as fast as we can with beautiful souls here on your Earth plane. Some who you have met before; you will think there are such a lot of coincidences, well you know they're not, they are all being orchestrated [in] a very fine way. Nothing that we do here in our world in Spirit is done haphazardly. It is very ordered, very orchestrated and you see the jigsaws, the pieces being put in, piece by piece.

So we thank you for all that you are doing, for all that you are doing for humanity and, of course, for the animal kingdom. And, of course, for Jimmy who we here in Spirit Love dearly as well.

So we will say good night and we will be back soon.

Thank you.

JUNE 23RD

Welcome and, although it's been a long time since we have been together, I have been with you, even in Greece.[53]

There are so many different things happening as I know you are aware. The first thing I need you to look at is the breathing techniques we sent to you. As I said to you that day, be aware we cannot do everything from this side; we are sending people to you.

Everyone that makes contact with you, by phone or in person, everyone that makes an enquiry, within your limitations I want you to follow these up because there are doors opening and paths leading.

The breathing techniques are very different and very special. I want you to weave those into the workshop. And also some of the material will come into the book. Also what's very important – it has always been but now more than ever – are the chakras. I want you to do a cleansing of the chakras on the course and, again as you read in the book[54] , what was brought to you from Spirit is the blending of the heart chakra and the throat chakra. This is very important [of] very high frequencies.

These are the frequencies that will help people through the turbulent times and will help with the dark energies. The symbol, I know that Anne is using the symbol, and has had some good healings with it, has two colours: green spirals represent the  heart centre, and the seven blue bars, the throat centre.

This is the healing symbol, an ancient healing symbol. I would request that people meditate on this particularly during and after the workshops, but certainly during the workshops.

I know that your workshop did not go ahead [the one planned for June 15th, in Volos, Greece] but Anne knew this was not the right time and not the right energy. Because of the energies that were going on at that time in that particular area of Greece.

But that will change, and workshops will be held over there, and will be held with Love and will be very successful.

I know you wondered at the time when I said I was very much like [David] Icke. There was a little bit of surprise from both of you. But I know, as you have seen things and heard things from him, you are realising we are saying the same thing. We are saying the same thing because it's coming from the heart.

It despairs me still that people are very troubled. But we know with the days and months that come, the energies are lifting. They are lifting now, and by the end of June the energies will get gentler. And things will start to slip into place. But there are a lot of [dark] energies and a lot of negativity through your media as you well know. We appreciate, here in Spirit world, [that] it is very difficult because whichever way you turn you are smashed with the negativity in the newspapers, the TV, the magazines, posters, whichever way. Rise above it, please rise above it.

As you know, once you get to the heart centre, to the energy within the heart, then the negativity will drop away. The dark energies can't feed on light energy. The heart energy is a light energy so it is very, very important you stay within this higher energy of light.

I know people are fearful of the coming months and some people think it is the end of the world. We know it is not, and we know you know it is not. It is a changing of energies and, although I can't tell you exactly what is going to happen, it will not be like anything that is being forecasted and is being fed to you.

A lot of the changes in energies started way back in the late 1980s and 1990s and now it is clearing out. And they are becoming finer and they are becoming more settled.

I know you have concerns for Greece. But as I have said before, Greece will come out of this far, far better and will be a much happier and wealthier country. Of course, nothing happens overnight but it has begun and people are opening their hearts and their minds and realising that there is a better way.

We need to go back now and speak about the chakra systems which I have said are very important. These draw in your life force energies and, while there is such negativity around, some of these energies will be slowing down. And when they slow down you will not be bringing in the life force the body needs, so it is important to look [at] and go through these energies. Anne knows how to do this, and I would recommend the two of you need to do it to make sure the vortices are spinning.

It will help with the tiredness you have been experiencing lately Jack. It is because of the changes of energy and your workload. Your workload must lighten and [you] must not look too deep[ly] into things. You have all you need, as much as you can for the Healing Code, and yes it can be tweaked and changed here but you basically have what you need. The Healing Code are a wonderful method of healing, more powerful than you'll ever know, and they have been brought in for this time to deal with the deep cellular, fearful memories that have been brought up from many, many moons ago.

The Diana workshops are going to be different. Of course, they are going to be [about] healing but they are going to be more tender and softer and gentler because people need these to be there. They need the gentleness of things, they need to feel the Love that will come from both of you as you do these workshops.

Go around and see what else is being offered, what other ways are coming into you. Miss nothing at the moment and look at things carefully. I know you talked about the Success Codes. The Success Codes will take their time and will attract people, but not like the Healing Code of course. But it is a nice combination and again it is working with the heart which we so badly need. So please, I would ask you to keep the Success Codes and to use them and to help people centre in the heart. These I think you will make simpler as time goes on.

The design of the ancient symbol is very important. I know at the moment that Anne is putting her concentration on this symbol. It goes back many, many times with deep healing. [It] was used by the Essenes for most of their work.

When people just look at this symbol they will feel a change in their energies. They will feel an opening of the heart chakra. And while we are on this point, I know that Anne had the heart chakra opened[55] while you were away [in Greece from 6-16th June] and that was very, very disturbing. But it had to happen; old energies had to go and this will be happening with other people, but not quite as profound[ly] as it happened to Anne. We needed to do this to clear out so that our lighter energies, our beautiful healing, higher evolved energies can come through.

We know we are putting a lot of pressure on her, and her energies are not as they should be, but this is because they are changing, and of the time, and it can only be done in this way. We are doing it as easily and as carefully and as gently as we possibly can. There will be work coming for you from Greece and that will be very beneficial and fulfilling for you.

I feel at the moment very concerned for your friend Vasiliki. I think she is very unhappy and concerned about her own circumstances. So we, here in Spirit, will be sending her Love and keeping her spirits up. She is a wonderful human being and so is Manos[56] and many, many other people you have met, not just in Greece but here too. And you know we are opening new doors for you… Ireland, where these places need Love and healing.

At the moment I am more concerned about the workshop next week [July 1st] and Anne has the format which I have given her over the last few weeks. I want you to look at that, and get the workshop in some order, although we do not know actually what will happen that day because we want to work with you with Love and light as is needed. But have no fears, you will all have a wonderful experience.

I want you to look at the breathing techniques. Now of course, Loukas, we orchestrated that for you.[57] There are no coincidences as you know. And I want you to look at the work he has brought for you and simplify it. And some of this will go in the book. Also, in the book, we should put in how beneficial the chakras are. And then when you have done the workshop, the book will come together for the total healing. There is not much more to do on the book, but the last few pages are vital.

I urge you, after the workshop, to get the book in some sort of order, and where you need to fill in with the likes of our very good healer friend here, Harry, who is with me often and he is one beautiful, shining soul.

There are many, many Spirits here in the Spirit world helping you and helping a lot of people. We really need the help that you are giving us and the help for humanity.

And, as David Icke says [and he is so right, and his heart has opened so much over the last 2 to 3 years, without David Icke this world would be a very different place], people are waking up, but yes he is right we are *Earth people*.[58]

Not human beings, being what? And doing what? Doing what for whom? The Establishment? The powers beyond? No, we are Earth people, and not everybody came from the Earth. Some of us came from the stars, from other galaxies. But basically we are Earth people, we blend with the Earth, and this is why now at this very time the chakras are so important.

They are bringing in information, vital information for you from the higher realms. And, of course, if these slow down you are not getting the information you need.

Know that you are powerful beyond belief. Some people can't and won't believe this, and it is understandable. For so long you have been hammered into the ground until some people feel they have nowhere to go any more. It is easier to stay hammered into the ground than to move forward, which can be very, very painful for a lot of people. To do that, they have to meet up with some of their old beliefs, their old hurts, and we understand how painful it can be.

But once they are accepted and faced then a new and brighter place [it] will be for you and all of mankind.

It is up to the likes of you to open the door, even if it is only a chink at a time, to let that light through, let the light of God come through and shine on people.

And once that happens, they will go forward, they will never go back to the dark times. We have to get rid of these dark energies once and for all. They have been around for thousands and thousands of years, getting darker and darker and darker. And if you can imagine what has happened to the planet, Mother Earth with billions of people living, breathing, feeling and seeing only darkness, feel what it has done to the Earth.

Here in Spirit, we are sometimes surprised as to how you have survived, although of course we're not! But, when we look at the darkness that you have been in, our hearts cry for you.

I want to talk a little bit again about the workshops.

You will find at these workshops that the people who come to you will be guided. They will have been with you before as a soul group. Very often with the Essenes, sometimes from Atlantis, but they will have been in your soul group. And the people that come will be very heart centred.

And our aim, and your aim is to open up and let them feel not my Love – though of course that will come through me and through to you – but God's Love.

To give these people an experience – even if it's just for one second – of the Love that they have never had before. It will open them up and make them search, and look far beyond where they are looking now. To look about their health, to look about the world with wonder, to go forward. Not to think about ageing; ageing is in the mind, but the mind will trick the body into believing things.

To the heart, and be at one in the heart.

We in Spirit are looking forward to your first workshop. We know there will be other Spirits, many Spirits around there next week helping you, being with you and we will be sending our Love so strong to open up the hearts of these people and your workshop.

I know that Jack was talking about using the symbol as a logo and we are pleased with that. We want people to see this logo, feel the Love that comes from it, meditate on it, hold it to the heart, put it in their hands because it has great power.

The more they use it, the more the power will be enhanced.

We are with you in Spirit, we are always with you. We will meet again next week once more before the workshop. In the meantime, I will still be giving Anne thoughts and images. Here in Spirit we want to see the sunlight in everyone's face once more and we want to see hearts opened, to see you standing in the light, absorbing the grace of God.

We can assure you that the energies are changing and people will start to feel a little bit lighter as we come to the end of June and go through to July. You won't feel the aches and pains in the body as you have, the sickness and the tiredness. It will get easier.

You need to stay with like-minded people to leave and bring the vibrations up as much as you can; stay in the higher vibrations, in the higher realms.

I will say to you now, it is time to get things in order as much as you can so that you are not as tired and not working as hard. Take short rests, the Diana workshops are going to go well; once you have the first one then we will give you more information. But we have to do it step-by-step because this energy is very, very high [and it may cause] some minor problems within the body.

I suggest the logo is used in all your material, business cards, slips all your material should incorporate this logo somewhere because it has power, it is beautiful and infused with Love. Do not underestimate it.

So, I'm going to leave you shortly, and I would like to wish Jack a happy birthday before I go. We in Spirit miss absolutely nothing, the Spirit world wish happy birthday to you. We will meet again next week.

CHAPTER FOURTEEN

JUNE 29TH

Well good evening. And it's great again to be back. Well. what a week![59] What a week in your world. What about the banks and the lies? I may say this is just the beginning of things.

We have been telling you this for a while now, and it is the start. The start of getting out all the old, all the lies, all the deceit. All the people that, for so long, have benefited for so long from your taxes, benefited from stealing from you. And it has to stop, and it will stop.

Your floods.[60] Do not be concerned about these floods. For although I know they are doing damage, it is only slight damage. And these floods are cleansing, they are cleansing Mother Earth. So welcome them, bless them, send them your Love knowing that as they are cleaning and cleansing Mother Earth needs this.

And you, with all the work you are doing, and the work you did in Greece and in other places that you are going, for everyone that you heal, for everyone that you shine your light on that is massive for us. It makes such a big difference here in Spirit and such a big difference to Mother Earth. She needs the Love and attention that you and your work give her.

I am greatly looking forward to your course and so are our Spirit friends here, and we will be with you. And I say 'we' because there are a lot of Spirit friends that will be coming. There are Spirit friends around you now. That is why you are itching [Anne was rubbing her ear]. We are excited about this, because this is quite new for you and quite new for us. We have drawn the people to you, the people that need to be there are the first ones to light the candles.

And do not worry about the course; it will be given to you. You have the bones of it, you have most of it and I have said look around you and test everything out because we are sending you things, and sometimes it may be in the most simple way and it can be easily overlooked and ignored.

You will get a flash, an inkling, and go with that feeling. As the time from around 6 July things will start to get a little bit easier and a little bit lighter. A lot of our work has now been done and has been being done prior to 1998. There is a lot of light now coming onto the planet, a lot of help from other species shall we say, not to frighten people. There is a lot of help from other galaxies. And of course, as you are aware, the reptilian race are stepping up and putting pressure on everything.

But the light will shine in the darkness and the bankers, and the politicians, and all the corrupt people that for so long have taken, and taken, and taken are now going to be exposed. It is their turn now, and it is your turn to reap some of the benefits these people have had for so, so long.

Healings you will be learning, and of course this is just the beginning, and we are just slowly giving them to you, but they are very powerful. The symbol is very powerful. It is ancient and it is the symbol of pure Love. And it brings the heart, and it brings the communication centre together. And when those two are working together all things, and I mean all things are possible.

People's hearts will be opened in a way that they have never been opened, and I know I said this about what had happened after my death, but on your course people's hearts will be opened differently and they will start to see and feel things differently. For some, they will get it easier than others. Make no bones about it, mark this, everyone will open up and everyone will feel a difference. And as they open up their hearts, it shines forth into the world.

And the heart chakra is very sacred; it is the engine of your body. So that once the heart is opened, it helps the body in many ways, it softens the arteries so the arteries don't become hard. It lets the blood flow, easily and freely. It helps the circulation and, as you know, there are a lot of illnesses related to bad circulation. The blood can be purified.

There is a lot of Spirit energy around you at the moment and we apologise because we know it is irritating *[Anne rubs her ear again]* you a little. We are bringing the energies in, so just bear with us.

They will feel very different after the Sunday course. They will feel lighter as their hearts open up, open up to Love the great healer, the great communicator. Time is now, 2012, as the energies change and Love flows into all the people on the planet. But some people will not understand this and so they will stay closed. But obviously the more people we can reach out to the better it will be for everybody and the planet.

I have said before that as things come to the forefront, as things, as the truth is being told there will be some unpleasant times. People will think they are going mad because, for all these years, they have been programmed and it is so ingrained into their thinking, into their way of being. So many things that really they don't know who they are. Because they have all these beliefs, beliefs of other people, of other generations. When they realise how everything has been lied to them, even the Bible, even the way the food is meddled with, even the way the monetary system has been so corrupt and for so long, even all the evil with paedophiles, some people will not be able to take this. And there will be suicides and some people, as I say, will feel they are going off their heads.

Because as with you, it has been drip fed over many, many years. And so you are aware of what is going on in the world. But you must also be aware that there are many, many people who are very closed. And these people are good people but they are very closed. And as everything is coming out, coming out with great force they will become overwhelmed with negativity. They will become very frightened, they will become very angry the way they have all been misled and their emotions will be so mixed that they will explode. And for some people it is going to be most unpleasant.

Some people will know that it is their time now to leave the planet; they have done what they needed to do and they will leave. And that's okay because there is no death, it is just a body. They have done what they came to do, and that's that.

It is difficult for you to believe that the world is going to be so much better. So much kinder, so much more Love. It is very difficult for some of you, I appreciate that, now when everything seems such a high state of anxiety, and insecurity. And we are doing it in the gentlest and the best way that we know for all humanity, but it has to be done, and it cannot be done without pain. We are working to ease the pain to the best of our ability. And things are coming in so quickly, it is quite overwhelming for you there on the Earth. And we know this. We are taking all the steps we can to be with you and to guide you.

There are more Angels and more Spirits on this planet now than ever. Doing their own work quietly and in their own way through the grace of God. To help the turbulent times to be calmer.

One day soon these times will be as calm as the sea, you will hardly be able to remember all that is going on at the moment. You see, everything has a cycle; nature has a cycle and if you put out and cheat and lie and steal and rape and pillage, yes you may get away with it for generations. But I tell you this, what you sow you truly reap. Nature, and the law it must be. That is the law, what you sow you reap. If you sow Love you will reap boundless Love in many, many ways. If you sow greed, and hate and lies and you cheat then imagine what you are getting back. It is unimaginable what will happen to these people.

They will not escape. The law of God is not cruel – it is fair and it is just – but it is the law.

It lifts our hearts to see the darkness coming out of your Earth. If you could see it here you would be very pleased. We can see the negativity rising up and coming out, being cleansed by the Love of God. And there are many, many people now opening up to spirituality. More than ever.

But although it has seemed slow and, as you know, there is no time here, in our time, but it is very much accelerating now. We are very pleased. The angelic realms are holding the world steady, are sending Love to the whole of the planet

When we looked at the Earth not long ago, it was cracked like Joseph[61] had said, it was cracked, and it was parched, and it was dry. But now it is changing back. Negativity is leaving, and Mother Earth is now being able to breathe again and her tears have dried. As the rains come and it cleanses and it nurtures the Earth, because the water, the rain is needed for Mother Earth because that helps cleanse negativity. And although it is unpleasant at times and you need the sun when you see it [the rain] know that it is cleaning and helping humanity.

If you were to see the energy around you when you are giving out Love from your heart you would absolutely dance with joy and now we see many, many of you with beautiful light around you. Yes, there are still the ones with dark clouds but there are so many more now on the path. On the path of enlightenment.

Do not be fearful of any extra-terrestrials from other planets. They have been here for many, many years helping you and have been circling your Earth thousands of years. You have so much help now, from all the spheres, from all the galaxies who are aware of what has been going on.

Stay within your power. As you are in the power of the heart, the power of Love, the negative energies cannot reach that vibration so it is so important that you stay within that higher frequency. Because they [the reptilians] cannot reach that higher frequency and as they feed off lower energies, lower frequencies then these negative energies will wither and die.

But over the past many, many hundreds of years they have thrived because of all the negativity. It did reach the peak where Mother Earth could not cope any more. But that is changing and she is beginning to breathe once more. And, as we do this and we breathe out Love from our hearts again, you will be able to breathe better within your own body system because the air will become better.

As you purify your air with Love it will help every living creature on the planet. You will find your vegetables and fruits will grow better because they thrive on the energy of Love, as every living being does. But we have been told the opposite. They have done everything to make you think and feel anything but Love. Because they know how powerful Love is. So they have orchestrated it all to go into a negative zone. Thankfully, people are now realising this and [are] changing.

So know we will all be with you on your workshop. Know that you will be guided, and know that the people there have been guided to you. As you know, you have had no problem filling that workshop. And once people have experienced the Love, and the Love they will get from me and you, and Jack they will tell others. So don't worry and don't fret about it. We are there to help you, all our Spirit friends will be there and the angelic realm. The energy will be very, very powerful; the energy will be very, very loving.

So go forward, with Love in your hearts, and do the work that God created you to do. To heal people, to heal the planet...

Chapter Fifteen

JULY 15ᵀᴴ

Welcome. It is good to be back here. Many things have happened since we last spoke, but here in the Spirit world we would like to thank you for the Diana workshop.

We are so pleased. And the energy and Love that was generated goes beyond our belief and our expectations. And we know you will carry on doing this work. The symbol is very powerful and, as I said, it brings the heart chakra and the throat chakra into line. You will have noticed as well, everywhere you seem to be turning you are hearing about the chakras. They have always been important but never as much as now. Because we are dealing with very different energies that you are both aware of.

I would suggest you regenerate your own chakras and align them. You will feel better and more alert and have more energy. And as these vortices are spinning and bringing in new life force energy it will have a great impact on your body. And, for the work you are going to do, you will need this. And, of course, with the energy changes within the atmosphere and in the planet.

There are many more changes ahead. Everything is breaking up, everything is speeding up to enable you to be more aware and deal with these new energies. Again, go back into your own well-being, meditation and into the chakra system.

As I said before, we cannot channel everything. It would take so much time on our parts and yours. We are sending information to you in many other ways. You have to be vigilant to see this, to hear it. Know for sure it is coming from here, from me and from all your Spirit friends, guiding you and taking you into other dimensions and other dimensions of energy.

The reason why Anne is feeling so tired at the moment [is that] her energies have been changing; her energies are becoming very active, very, very powerful. With all the energy that was in the room yesterday, her energy overload was possibly a little too much. But this will align itself in the next three or four days; things will start to improve in the energy levels.

I know Anne thought the course didn't go as well as it could have done yesterday[62] and maybe as you look at it as it happened, maybe in your eyes it didn't. But there was great healing and great learning there for everyone. So please do not condemn yourselves for this. And I know, as Jack said earlier, it may be preparing the way for other healings that you will have, because you are going to have some challenges. There are people that are so ill, so desperately ill both physically and mentally and, as I have said before, this is going to just grow. People cannot deal with the changing of the energies – as things are evolving rapidly and the truth is coming out – they are going to be so let down and so disappointed and feel threatened and insecure.

So that will affect their mental health and that will turn into physical problems if they don't deal with it. So you will be having more people coming to you [with] more challenges.

The path that is laid out is quite straight for you. [People] will come to you particularly for the workshops. We are sending people to you of the right calibre, people who have been in our lifetimes before. There is nothing here that I haven't said before.

I know that you are planning to go to Greece. Do not be surprised if you are asked to do a Diana workshop at the Hotel. It is a possibility. So just be aware of that. It is entirely up to you of course whether you do it, we in Spirit here will never push you to do anything.

The symbol, as we said before, although I know that you would have thought of it, yes the idea of the necklace or pendant we would've brought that through anyway. We did in fact through Jan [see notes 24 and 70]. We need you to get on with this now. We need you to get on with this now. The vibrations are very powerful and people will feel wonderful healings from it and will have faith in it. They will trust it and they will trust you. I know already that people do trust me and that is why I came through to you. We need that trust on all sides.

And I know at first you thought it was all quite strange. But, as I explained, it was because people trust you, [and] care about you. There may be other people that they will not trust as they do you. You would be amazed how many people trust you and Love you and sometimes you can't see that, you can't see the wood for the trees.

But this is now rippling out, rippling out slowly, you think, but underneath there are undercurrents; people are talking about it. It won't take too long. I want to say to you please get yourselves in order both physically and mentally, and get your affairs in order as much as you can, because when this work starts to really ripple out you will have very little time for yourself. You know that already and you are committed to this.

We know that you have had challenges, lots of challenges in the past 2 to 3 years and we appreciate that has possibly taken its toll. Things are improving, and things will turn around as I know you are aware. You have been told many times things will turn around and start to progress for you.

The world at the moment, in so many people's eyes, seems such a mess, and indeed it is. But we here in the other world are working silently, dutifully and with people in many, many other countries; working on their energies and their beliefs. While sometimes it may seem very depressing to see some of the pictures that you see, hold your spirits up, hold your hearts up and know that changes are happening and probably quicker than you imagine.

I have spoken before about David Icke and he is doing a wonderful job. And also all the offshoots that have come now and all the other people that are coming in and supporting David Icke and his Truth movements. Everything is growing, and growing, and growing and again rippling out [to] such a degree, much faster here than we thought it would in the Spirit world. So we are well pleased with all that work.

Know that there are many ways that you are being manipulated and you do have to protect yourself. Try to go up into the higher vibration of Love, Love from the heart, go within the heart and be careful of the mind. The mind will trick you now more than ever because they are finding ways to play and to activate the mind, negative ways. And yes, we have talked about thoughts being yours and you know you are going into collective consciousness and not all thoughts are yours.

Some of these [toxic] thoughts are being put out purposely so [that] people feel fear, more fear. Fear of their own well-being, the fear of everything, and as you know security[63] is top of the list.

I ask you this question 'Who do you know that wants to kill their neighbour? Who do you know that wants to kill their friends? Who do you know that wants to slaughter children?' These thoughts are being put in people's minds, these thoughts are being put in minds by medication.

People will stop at nothing to gain power.

But you have more help than you will ever know. You have more help from here, the Spirit world, and also from your friends called the 'aliens'. You have been learning today not to be fearful of all you hear and read. I know you are very selective in what you hear and watch but nevertheless they have ways they can get to even the most alert people. They are stopping at nothing, they are running in fear and they are using every technology they possibly can [to instil] total fear.

And this is why it is so important for the work you are doing. You must look at ways now to really push this Diana work out. And the Healing Code. We are bringing people to you and there are so many people out there wanting to help you. Do not be afraid, push this work out.

We are giving you proof. We gave you proof last week when people saw me transformed from you to me and from me to you.[64] So do not be afraid, we are with you here, we are with you if people criticise and mock. Know all the power here in Spirit world is more powerful than any of your power on the Earth plane.

We will change this planet, and change it to one of Love and harmony. Thank you for all you're doing.

And I was so pleased because yes, the first time I did contact you, you had that beautiful verse from that unknown person. [65] That was our first point of contact and bringing our hearts together. Though it did not make sense at the time we had to be sure ourselves that we had chosen the right person and at the time we knew you were going through many trials to make you stronger. And although you may not feel that, I can assure you that you are stronger in so many ways, you would be amazed.

We need to step this up now; we will help you here and send people to you. Go forth. Hold, your head up high. You have been chosen and you have passed.

Jack I think you have some questions?

I do Diana, and congratulations on your birthday on July 1.

Thank you.

And now I'm beginning to feel your presence. I haven't seen you yet but there again that isn't a problem for me, but I can certainly feel your presence. I can feel it at the moment. The breathing material that you allowed us to have. We used a simpler version on the workshop and there is a more complicated version. Should we promote and use the more complicated version?

The answer to that is yes. But, I would say, integrate it more slowly because to bring the whole lot in may be so overwhelming for some people. Just look at it carefully and you will see when you start to devise this to make it slightly simpler because breathing, as you know, is so important. It is the breath of life, it is God within us. This is a beautiful way of clearing the conscious mind of turmoil and the body of toxins and so it takes you into a higher dimension. So it is very important the breathing. Very, very important.

I think what you did on the first day was absolutely magnificent. The whole day we were there, Harry, and Jesus and myself, many Angels and many other beings, many other people that are so proud of you in your family were there.

know that we will never let you down in any way. Sometimes, as I said earlier, it may not go according to plan, your plan, but rest assured it is going according to our plan. So do not beat yourself up in any way when things happen or things appear to be out of sync. They are not out of sync; they are totally in sync. Does that make sense to you?

I realise that. I realised that some hours ago.

Sometimes it may seem a little bit difficult but we have to remember some people themselves are hurting so deeply inside it is hard to express, and sometimes their response and their anger is their deep, deep hurt. And I know you and Anne are very aware of this but sometimes it can shake you a little. And you may wonder, had you done the right thing? You can only do the right thing because you are coming totally from the heart. Sometimes, [for] the person you may be healing, this is their lesson. The total purpose of the healing they need to learn themselves.

I now realise that. I didn't realise it at the time but I'm really grateful for the experience. Another question I'd like to ask you. We are currently reading the work of Bob Frissell,[66] I just find it incredible. I'm assuming he is one of the people you have either directed to us or us to him. Have you any comments?

Yes, we are directing people to you and his work is absolutely wonderful. And in his work there is so much that you need. Although you do know *[about what Bob says in his books]*, but just to confirm that some of these things that are going on are being said by him and by other people as well. Take from his books what you need, because we are sending the right people to you. As I say, if we had to channel all these people and their workings it would take 100 years and we haven't got that time anyway. We must go forward, forward from the heart. Show people that there is Love out there for them even when they are feeling so frightened and scared. Just to give them that first touch of Love on the hearts that will open up.

Once their hearts are open, very quickly they will begin to heal in many more ways than they realise.

Another question I have, a slightly deeper one this time, is about having free will on the Earth plane – and all I can say is thank God we do – but we also have help from the Spirit world, and from yourself and other sources. I wonder how I might reconcile having free will and the influence, the necessary influence, that is coming from the world of Spirit and our friends from other planets?

But you still have free will and we are here to help and guide you. You are never forced at any time to do anything that you do not want to do. You have a choice, but your heart knows that choice and we have to leave it there because you have to choose for yourself. Some of your path is planned, as you well know, before you come back into the body and this path was planned. You will have free will to step off it if you so wish. Any time, you can take the decision to just stop what you're doing. We cannot, no matter how evolved we are, we cannot interfere with your free will. But what we can do, once you are open to us and give us permission, [is to] help you with all the Love and blessings that we can. Is that clear for you?

Completely. And I wouldn't have any other path.

Good.

One last question. We are coming to the end of the book.

Yes we are.

And I know we will get a publisher, I trust you 100%; just occasionally I get frustrated but then I know once a certain stage is reached we will get that. Any insights or any suggestions would be greatly welcomed.

I feel that there are two publishers who would be interested in the book. You really have to 'fish the seas', and again the Yellowfin is coming back and a smaller publisher. The name of Kingfisher. And in the meantime cast the net wider to where you think there are publishers that would not be interested, where you have sort of 'blanked' them in a way. Is there anything else?

No. I always smile because there are so many questions I would have asked but you've already answered them, so from me it is sufficiently today and I'm eternally grateful for these sessions.

Well we will have another one or maybe two but I know Anne is extremely tired and it is getting difficult. So with all our Love here in Spirit we will say our goodbyes. Bless you until we meet again.

Chapter Sixteen

July 27th

Welcome. It's so good to be back. And this will not be the last [channeling] obviously because I'm in communication with Anne daily – many times during the day.

Lots of things to talk about – certainly my concern and I know your concern – is the children. And I know it's been in your media about children of four or five being destructive in schools. This is where – as we have said – that unless these children are given Love, unless they are shown an alternative, then we fear for the future.

But we know this will change, we know it [the message of Love] is spreading now and although you may feel it is taking a little while, we want to get this right. And I promise you, it will not take long. Hearts will be opened and people will learn how to love their children. But, you see, they have never been loved themselves. So it is quite a huge task, but a task that will ripple out and we thank you, and we thank all your friends that have helped you get the workshops.

I know you have just had a picture of the symbol, which I'm so delighted about, so, so pleased about that I just want to burst into laughter and Love, because the symbol is more important than you probably realise. It carries a beautiful energy, the energy of healing, the energy of Love and it will do you and serve you well. Everybody that wears it or comes into contact with it will feel that energy.

Again I know we have the Olympics.[67] We shudder here in the Spirit world; we shudder with what is going on. But people are becoming aware and, in one way, [when] we are shuddering we are jumping with joy in the other direction. People are aware, not only in this country, but in America, all over the world. People are aware of what is going on. They understand the symbols; they understand the power of the symbols, the negative symbols that I am talking about now.

Pour out your hearts; shine your light on this evil place, with these evil symbols. And let us turn this world around, because it can be done and it will be done. But it can only be done with the right intentions and with Love, and caring and sharing for each other.

Until we can learn that – and it is happening – we have no doubt here in Spirit that it is happening, really quicker than we anticipated. Although it's never quick enough for us but we realise you are human and you have your human daily duties to go through.

But I know the energies are changing, and I know that you are feeling them. And in the last few days these energies have changed quite dramatically.

Do not be upset about what has happened in the last few days.[68] It was not meant to be, and we made sure it would not happen. It would not have been a happy time for you. And although it seemed a good offer at the time and probably was, there were things that were not right there and people had their own difficulties to deal with. It would not have been the right venue or the right time. So we take you away from that place and we will take you back to that area – but not that particular place – when the time is right. You will have offers of other work coming in from other directions for the Diana workshops and of course the Healing Code. This will grow and this will blossom, and either one of the courses will bring Love and give nourishment and cherish people and that is what it's all about.

They have to learn because people are hiding behind their shadows. People are not hard or cruel. The majority of people that is of course; we do have the odd minority. The majority of people are just lost; they don't know where to go and, of course, there is confusion in the mind. And that is meant to be. You are given good news, then bad news, then good news, then bad news. It is mind games, mind games, total mind games.[69] So that most of the people are so confused they don't know which way to go; they don't know what to believe.

So we have to get the truth [out]. The truth will always stand up, the truth will stand up to scrutiny no matter what. And we in Spirit are behind you and you will see this grow. You are attracting lovely people like Jan.[70] She is working so hard for you and for us here in spirit; she is one beautiful soul. And we will attract more 'Jans' to you. And it is happening already, so do not despair at that 'little' incident.

And I say little because I know, at the time, it was quite hurtful and upsetting but to us it was a little incident that was to go nowhere.

Over the next few weeks, three to four weeks there will be changes, changes in the planet and people will feel that little bit happier and I might even say a little bit of joy.

We are doing all we can here in Spirit. We are working with you and again we are working with the dark side. Because we are shining our light there and people are coming to the front, people we call, or you call 'whistle-blowers'. Eventually things will change in such a way, and so quickly, you will not be able to draw breath. And you will understand, as many people do but billions do not. This is where you come in, and your friends, and your disciples, and the people coming tomorrow and that will come in the future, you have a job to do. Helping these people stay here if they wish to, or helping them go back to the world of Spirit. And some will choose to go, they will not be able to take it any more.

So, we are working with it. We are, as we have promised, being with you and helping you all the way. And when things do go a little bit wrong, just trust in us, we will be there. Because they don't 'go wrong', they just show you another way.

I'm so glad that you like the breathing techniques,[71] we couldn't have channelled that, don't think I could have channelled that. You know what they call me,[72] well however we will leave that one, Jack knows what I mean! It was much easier to do it through the channels that we did. And it is so important because sending light into Mother Earth you are cleansing and empowering her and she needs that, and she is so grateful. So the more people we can get to do this, cleanse the Earth, give Love to Mother Earth, give her new vital energy that is needed at this time that will make such a big, big difference.

There will be probably more little things to come, but again we need now to get [to] the close of the book. And I don't feel there is much more we can add other than that we are all with you here in Spirit. You must never despair, no matter how dark it might seem. Hold on, we are there and we will be working with you. As one door closes, many will open. We will be with you always, always, always.

And although it may not feel that way at times, as you open doors to help, be it one, be it 101, be it 1,000,001 it does not matter; you are doing the work that you came on this Earth to do. As so are many of the people that now are coming to you. So trust in God, trust in us, we are all working to the one end.

I know that Jack has some questions.

Thank you Diana, I have a number of questions. You had already anticipated one and have answered it. What I'm finding, as you know I do the research, a body of information, a body of knowledge that is being captured in this vehicle called the 'Healing Revolutions.' [73] *We are concentrating on the moment, and rightly so, on your workshops and on the Healing Code. But I still feel there is a purpose to these other workshops.*

If it is flowing to you, it is being sent to you from us in Spirit. While you have the Diana workshops and the Healing Code the Healing Revolutions must continue. There is different work in that, no more powerful than anything else you are doing, but you see we have to attract different people to different things. And some will be attracted to the Healing Code, some to the Diana workshops, and some to the other work you are doing. The more variety you can give people, hey let's get on with it!

Thank you. The other question was, yes the book is nearly finished it is getting to that stage, you did say there would be other books. I'm wondering when we will begin the second book?

I'm not sure on this but I would think towards the end of the year or the turn of the year because I think you have so much work to do between now and then and different things will be coming in. I feel as well [that] the last 12 months have been quite traumatic for Anne and yourself. But particularly Anne with the different changes of energies. Her energies are still changing and they are getting more and more powerful. She will have to deal with that, we will help her and she will go and get through it all. But it will sometimes be quite profound and different. And very high energy can also sometimes take your energy as it settles around you.

So, although I will be communicating in a different way, the channelling may just stop for a little while. We'll see how things go. We want to give you breathing space. But again, if Anne makes notes of what is coming in on a daily basis that will help to maybe start the other book. I just want you to be able to breathe and get on with your work now, to get it all out as quickly as you can. Is there anything else?

Yes, thank you again Diana. In the Bob Frissell book, there is reference to 're-birthing.' [74] *There are two elements to re-birthing as you know, there is the breathing process which you have guided us to incorporate into the Diana workshops and there is also the clearing up of emotional cellular memory. It is my view that the Healing Code, enhanced by the Diana work and the symbol is even more powerful than what Bob was dealing with 20 years ago.*

You are absolutely right, you are so right. This energy, along with the symbol now is coming in. We need a stronger energy. I mean, the work that he has done is absolutely fantastic and it has found its way to you and Spirit have coordinated that. When you ask for things from Spirit, sometimes we can do it straight away, sometimes we have to work through things and remove things and bring in things and sometimes it can take a little while. But you have hit the nail on the head; you have got all that you need there and anything extra will come in to your other work. There is nothing more to say because you have it all there. You will do research and add to it, you will take feedback from your courses and results, and change them as you have done. And carry on doing that because, as you know, energy and new ideas are coming in all the time. But I will tell you it will be a little while before anything comes in as strong as the Healing Code and the work you are doing with Diana. In fact it will be quite a while before anything new will come in. Yes, new stuff will come in but it has a long way to go before it gets to reach the power of the Healing Code, the Diana work and some of the other stuff you are bringing in.

Thank you Diana. Just one last question which is a personal one. I had a near death accident in 1977 [75] and I have no memory of that, nor do I wish to have one. But I'm wondering if, it may be just completely wrong, I was a 'walk-in' or I changed as a result of that?

I would say that you are not a walk-in. But when you were out of consciousness then your energy and your power changed within that time. And that power changed to get you more into the work you are doing now.

That makes sense.

Does that help you?

Absolutely.

I know that Anne laughed last week when John Lennon[76] appeared at her side, but she was not imagining this. I always loved John Lennon and I loved the Beatles, but John Lennon in particular was very special and could we say – haha – John was before his time. Some of his work, and some of his words were very ahead of [their] time and he frightened a lot of people because he was so powerful. A lot of people didn't understand it, they just thought they were words and lyrics in songs, but no – they were so powerful and I know, as you are listening to them now, you will be understanding it more. And John is here and we work together; we are [of a] very, very similar frequency and don't be astounded if other people come in as well. Now we have got this communication with you, we will not make a mockery of it, we will not mock you, we will not bring people to you that are not deserving of you.

But John was so taken, and he wanted to come through and, as he said to Anne, he feels an affinity to yourself Jack.

Very similar in a way that you were, he was adopted in some way by his aunt; his parents didn't want him. And the working class hero...all the things he felt quite a strong attachment to your heart. Just take these things on board, you will find a few more of our friends coming in, but be aware. If we send them, what I ask you to do, and Anne has been doing this, ask for protection from Archangel Michael. Yes there are imposters, and they are growing bigger and faster because obviously, they want to trick you and they have ways of doing this. But always ask Archangel Michael for protection before you enter our kingdom, the Spirit world, so that you know you are protected. You will only bring through then the good Spirits like myself, John Lennon and Michael Jackson, Spirits that have got an affinity and work from the heart. So don't be thinking we are making a mockery of it should we bring some of our very close and dear friends. We are working in unity here and in Love and that's all that matters and we need to get the right people.

And, as I have said, we took time choosing you, and yes, it seemed odd, you know a much older couple not interested in the Royal family. Oh yeah, we laugh at that. Not interested in me, not interested in the clothes I wore! Well, we'll leave that one with you Jack... I don't need clothes are any more you see, they can have it all as they say!

Humanity needs the greatest help since it began. Things are coming to the forefront, liars and cheats are being found out and that lifts our hearts here in Spirit. And it will happen more daily, daily. Two or three times a day things will come now to the surface and they will not be able to hide behind their money, their fortunes, their cars, and their swanky houses. No, no, no. That, for a lot of people is coming to an end, and yes they will need help. Because they have deluded themselves for so long by thinking that all they needed was higher education, money, things, possessions, mansions, swimming pools, planes – you name it – well, that brings them no power. There is only one power in this world and that is the Love of God and without that they are no-thing. Nothing. And so they can buy people, but that only lasts for so long, and they have to come back when they reincarnate again. So a lot of those people will absolutely be in total terror and trauma, and again they may come to you. And I know, with an open heart you will help these people. They are, after all, human beings with hearts that have just got into this perpetual circle of greed.

So, open your hearts to all and sundry, they will need it, knowing you are protected. And while we know you have attracted, and sometimes helped, people and opened their hearts they have not perhaps exchanged that in the long run. That will not happen now. We have opened your heart but we have also protected it, and so go on and push yourselves forward. The time is right; push yourselves forward with Love and gratitude. We are with you here always. Any more questions Jack?

No more questions Diana, and thank you again. Just one comment. Could you thank John [Lennon] for his comments about me. I feel privileged – words fail me – to have a connection with someone like John Lennon as I do with you.

Well, we don't know where these connections are going to end up, but think big. Think big, think outside the box, think with Love, be Love. Because all those people with

151

power, as I have said, they are no-thing. They have no power, they think they have power. They have no power. There is only the Universe, and the universal God that has the power. But yes, they have a certain amount of power to try and destroy the human race, but oh what little minds? Because they are the human race! Does it not cross their minds for one minute that if they destroy you, they destroy themselves and their families? It is just unbelievable. It is unbelievable that power and greed will force you and push you to even destroying your own family! God help them, because they are going to need it. But now, as you would say Jack, off my soap box.

We will leave you in peace, we will leave you in Love, and we will leave you to carry on your good work with our help. And John is just coming here, sends his Love and gratitude, and he says 'do one thing for me, send Love to Yoko'.

And from that, we will bid you farewell and we will come back to you when the time is ready. So blessings to you and everyone, and blessings to the people tomorrow. Give them our gratitude and Love and I know that Anne thought 'I won't mention it about John Lennon.' Please do, he wants you to. He says you are going back to his homeland or near his homeland. Take his Love and my Love to that area and let it shine.

We Love you all, we are with you all and we will come back. You haven't got rid of us yet so good night and thank you.

JULY 12TH 2013

You will notice that nearly a year has elapsed since the previous channelling. However, much has happened in the intervening period. Anne set up her YouTube channel as a home for Diana's twice monthly channelling in December 2012 and a month ago we agreed a deal to have this book published before the end of this year. Anne's first workshop channelling was recorded on [Diana's birthday] July 1st 2012 and appeared on Jack's YouTube channel.

In October 2012, we visited the ancient city of Delphi, in Greece.[77] At this most spiritual and significant of places, Anne did a channelling, which you can also see on Jack's YouTube channel. Two remarkable things emerged. Firstly that I (Jack) had been one of the builders of Delphi, which goes a long way to explaining my passion for the country. Secondly, you are referred to Chapter 3. Diana had previously said she had been 'connected to' Artemis the Greek/Roman goddess.

Was Artemis a real person? In the museum at Delphi is a mask, the picture of which I saw in a book about the place. Anne is very reluctant to share this information, but if you look at the mask you will see an incredible likeness between Artemis and Anne. And Diana's observations? Anne was Artemis...

Back in the UK, we 'stumbled across' somewhere we had passed through fleetingly a few years previously. Malvern in Worcestershire. A truly beautiful place with special energies and a host of other attributes you should discover yourself. We subsequently discovered Malvern was the source of inspiration for authors J R R Tolkien (Lord of the Rings) and C S Lewis (The Chronicles of

Narnia). It inspired composer Sir Edward Elgar. There is a statue of Elgar in the town centre.

Visiting Malvern had an effect on both of us. We came back a few times. We planned to run some workshops here. And then we 'decided' to move here. Our house in Cheshire was sold before it went on the market in February 2013. Complications with the buyer's financing meant that the completion of the sale took far longer than expected.

Who do you think might have been Diana's favourite composer, whose music she turned to at times of despair? You guessed it, Elgar. And when do you think the sale of our house was completed? Right again, Diana's birthday, July 1st.

The last piece of relevant detail here is that at a psychic development circle session in April 2013, Anne had been told by the circle leader, Carol Dunning (a great friend, and amazing clairvoyant), that one final chapter of the book was waiting to be written.

Before you read this chapter, Malvern will be the location of the Diana Divine Healing Sanctuary, which we trust will be 'open for business' in 2014. The (yet another incredible) story of how that came about is for another book.

And need we say any more about what's going on in the world in terms of awakening, oppression and things coming to the surface? What an amazing time to be alive!

Well good evening, and this evening is to re-cap and go further with the book. There is just a little more finishing off that needs to be done. It is several months since we have done work for the book, but we have channelled much more.

I would like to say thank you to everybody who has lifted their vibration up, and this world is starting to change. So much has happened in the last 12 months, and [some of] you may say

'Well what?' If you could see here as we can in the world of Spirit, you would see there are so many positive changes within your world. As I have said to you many times, the truth will always come out, the truth must always be told, and I said this would start to happen and you are aware that it is.

There is a lot more to come out yet, it may be quite startling and it may be quite frightening, but know that it has to come out. And people are saying 'Why is it taking so long, what is happening? Have Spirit forgotten us, are they leaving us here?' Well of course not. It cannot be cleared so quickly because it goes back so many thousands and thousands of years. All the dark negative energies, all the resentments, all the hurts that have been buried for thousands of years are now coming to the forefront, and the healing is taking place in many beautiful ways.

So, please do not feel that Spirit are not working with you. I promise you we are. And we are proud of what you have achieved, attained in just a short while. And I say keep together in your groups; I've said this many, many times because as you speak with positive words, the vibration is higher. The higher the vibration, the less the negative energies can get in and affect you. And people may say, 'How can the world be better when there is so much negativity, so much anger?' When you look to certain countries, that are now uprising, there is so much anger. Well of course there is so much anger. It has been buried for generations, and generations, and generations. And when people come to realise, how they have been fooled, how things have been faked, of course it will make them angry and hurt, and depressed.

Because you have all been hoodwinked for generation, after generation, after generation.

So it does take time to clear. But it is going at a much faster pace than we ever thought it would. Earth, Mother Earth is beginning to breathe again. As you remember when we first started the channelling [January 2012] I was very concerned about Mother Earth. She was broken and parched. And the energy was drained out of her. But slowly, slowly she is coming back to life. Back to the force of nature. Well you may say, 'What about the GMO foods?' Well indeed it is a curse in many, many ways. And I have said many, many times watch what you are eating and take responsibility. Be careful of what you are eating, and to say no to these foods. Countries are saying no, and of course if there are no takers, then of course it will diminish and die.

And I have said that Mother Earth is strong, and resistant. And nature can soon come back to the fullness that the Earth provides for all. And I have said go and grow your own food. It is so pleasurable in doing that. And you know, insofar as you can know, that food will not have been tampered with. Buy the organic seeds. Do the very best you can, because nothing, nothing can be 100%, we know that. But if you do your best, by buying the best, you will reap the rewards as you eat the food you have sown and grown yourself.

And again, bless the food. Ask God, thank God for the food that nourishes you and keeps you alive. The food that is on your plate every day, just bless it with the Love of God. Your food will taste better, and the harmful chemicals will be released.

So, there are many, many ways you can help yourself. All is not lost, as the people who run your planet would have you believe. All is not lost indeed – all is just about to waken up – going forward with new strength, new vitality and Love.

And you ask about the wars. Yes we watch, we watch with horror at what each country is doing to each other. And I ask you not to dwell, not to feel anger and hatred and resentment towards the people in the wars. It is easy to judge, it is easy to condemn. You are not told the truth. And by you being angry and being resentful you are just making matters worse, and feeding it with negative vibrations. So send Love to the people in the war. People who've set these wars in motion will have to pay one day, that is for sure. But the more you send your anger and hatred out, the more they will feed on your negative energy. So again, send your Love to them and bless them. Yes, war is all about money – make no mistake about it – money is always the root cause. In the wrong hands of course, money can have dreadful consequences. But I would say don't condemn money; money can be used by many people in so many positive ways.

I was very fortunate because I came from a privileged background, and so for me, money was not a problem and money was not important because it was always there. But I realise many of you are struggling from day-to-day, and some hour-to-hour. Have faith and hold that faith in your heart and ask and pray. Every prayer gets answered, every single prayer. And though that might sound unbelievable, I assure you every prayer gets answered. Maybe not in the way you think, but your needs will be met.

We see the world [as] so beautiful, so different from yourselves, because of course we are not in your reality; we are not in your dream. Dream, but dream the positive dreams, dream about the world you want to see, of the beautiful, picturesque trees and flowers and beaches. There are so many beautiful things on your Earth, so focus on the beauty, not the negativity of the Earth, not the wars but the beauty that is around you daily. Notice it, and give gratitude to the Creator God for giving you all these beautiful, beautiful things.

There are many great changes happening, some are quiet and subtle; some will be perhaps a little frightening. But know they have to happen so that you can have the world that is there already and waiting for you. A world where people care, and Love each other, a world without all the illness, a world without all the wars, a world without the poverty. Where every need will be met and, in fact, is met. As the higher vibrations change on the planet these higher vibrations change in you because we are so connected to the planet. We are part of the planet and, as all this changes, your energy will change. You will become freer and lighter, and healthier. And I would say, if everybody could only realise how simple it would be to change, and to change the world and the happenings around you, you would be astonished.

If you remember, we are all one. All connected. And what you do to your brother you are doing to yourself. And if everybody carried that with them – that if they resent someone, they are resenting themselves – that if they harm someone, they are harming themselves. How can it not be if we are all connected? And if we are all connected to the one Creator, and we are all connected to the planets, and the stars, everything in your body is connected to the whole Universe. You are the Universe, and the Universe is you. And as soon as people realise [that] what they do to another person [will] come back to them, how different things would be. If people thought, before they hurt another living thing, they are just but hurting themselves, how easy it is to change your world.

Can you understand that, can you see that?

By sending Love to someone who you are perhaps not on good terms with, instead of the negative thoughts of wanting to hurt them, start to send thoughts of Love and care. That will affect your body, and it will also affect their body. And if we all remember we are all one, then life on Earth will change very, very quickly. If you can imagine we are all vibration, we are all energy, then if an animal in another part of the world, say an elephant, shakes his or her ears then that vibration travels. Then that vibration affects us, very subtly and very slowly. We don't even notice. But everything that happens in all four corners of the Earth affects each and every one of you. And so surely, surely think about your future generations and your children. Surely it is so much better to give out kindness and compassion and Love instead of hatred and resentment. Even as you speak the words you will feel the different sensations of energy in your body.

So we know that it takes time, because for so long you have been programmed with negative thoughts, and told negative things. Most of those are untrue. But if you turn everything-shall we say on its head-and know what you've been told is the opposite. The truth will make such a big difference – start to understand how you can change this planet. You have the responsibility; it is no use leaving it to your next door neighbour, your friend or the man across the road. You have the power, you have the responsibility. And when you get into the vibration of Love and compassion and caring you are powerful beyond belief. Do not believe me, try it and see the difference. It will change your life, and the people around you.

Go forward with Love in your heart, and take this planet into a higher loving vibration that will change the lives of every man, woman and child and every living thing on planet Earth.

Do you have any questions Jack?

I was thinking about having a Diana prayer to use when heal-
ing, similar to the Healing Code prayer, and then I realised we
already have one. I just say the first four lines, so would I be right
in assuming that this is the prayer to use?

That was given to Anne, although at the time she had no
idea, why should she? That was the first thing I wanted to
give [to her]. There is so much power in that prayer. It came
from the world of Spirit with all the Love that you can bring
into a prayer, and it brings a new energy, and I am pleased
that you are using the prayer. And offer it to everyone.

Thank you. I am quite a fan of some people on the Internet who
use anger as a tool to wake people up,[78] but I wouldn't want to take
it further because I'm in 100% agreement that hatred and resent-
ment gets us nowhere. As a tool to wake people up, is anger useful?

Well it is indeed, because how can you wake people up
softly, softly? Sometimes the hard truth has to be shown and
talked about. By shouting in that way, not the way I was
meaning, people hating each other with anger and resentment, to wake up the sleeping people, to me it is a wonderful,
valuable tool. You cannot wake people up by whispering in
their ear. And so it has to be done in various different ways.
Does that answer your question?

Perfectly. You have been directing a number of people to us in
the last few months, all wonderful people. Are there any ones in
particular that we should give greater attention to?

Well I think you give and spend all your Love and energy
to everyone who comes your way, even people that you have
never met, and that's wonderful to do. I would say perhaps
your friend Gary[79] is in need of some loving and caring for
the moment. But I never think about singling people out,

because I know you will do that, so I don't have to think about it. I know that every person who comes your way that needs help will get it, and will get it 110%. So yes, I, Spirit are sending people to you, people will find their way to you, because we trust and we know you will do the work. And remember you can only do your very best. And I know that Anne gets stressed when people don't heal as quickly as she would like them to, but that is not in your hands. Your task is to administer the healing with Love and care and the rest is up to Creator God. OK?

You mentioned before the insanity about people harming others because they're harming themselves, but as I'm sure you know a lot of people don't like themselves, a lot of people resent themselves. So criticising others and harming others is OK because it's the way they see themselves. Is there any way to break out of that prison?

They've been programmed to hate themselves.[80] They have been programmed for generations and each generation hates itself a little bit more. And they are told [the same thing] by their teachers and their peers. And for people who come to you then, the people [and there are many millions of them] I can only say what I've been saying over and over again, send them Love from your heart – you don't need to know them – and send Love to the groups. Because what you do by asking for the Love of God to enter their hearts is so powerful I can't express it to you. It is a power of Love beyond your understanding on the Earth plane. And it's not going to happen overnight, we've said this before, but the journey has started and it is well on its way.

So as you see these groups, maybe on your television screen, the Internet, send your blessing and Love to them. Send Love out, because they have been so trodden on that they don't know what they're doing, they don't realise, and as they turn their hatred on to others, and they wound and hurt, they are hurting themselves more. It will come back to haunt them, the more it goes on.

The law of the Universe is that things have to even out; the more you do you will get paid back whether good deeds or negative deeds. It has to be. It has to be black-and-white. It has to be. It has to be balanced. The law of the Universe will do that. So, it's hard when what you see on your screen is people hacking each other, it's hard. It's hard to understand how one human being can do that to another. We find that hard in Spirit. How can you ever, ever act like that? What we have to do, we have to forgive, and start to Love and care and break this mould.

And there are more of you with Love in your hearts than without.

It's just waking up the people to say 'Hey come on, you have Love in your heart, you can give.' And as you know yourself, we have spoken many times about this. It doesn't take millions, it takes but a few in the great big picture of things.[81] And you are awakening people, and many other light workers are. And you can see the great changes that are happening, the truth is coming out; your whistle-blowers. I told you this two years ago. And people will realise, and they will come together, in ways you have never seen, never seen for thousands of years. So just keep working, keep going on, keep going forward. Keep ploughing your seeds of light and Love, wherever you go. And that goes for the like-minded people like yourselves. We can see these seeds of light and Love lighting the planet with Love and light, changing the energy in ways you will never really know. And you have many helpers here from Spirit and from the angelic realms. They are all around you now this evening. The Angels are coming closer to the Earth. So pray for these people, pray that their hearts of stone will be softened and that they will realise the way they are is not the way, it will only bring more suffering and violence. And you know it is only a handful of people in the great picture that are doing these things. It is not as it is made out, that one country is fighting another country, it is just a small handful [of people] but you are never told that. You are never told the truth; you are led to believe that the whole country is fighting another whole country. And it is not that way, you know that, many people know that, but many people believe what they hear and see [from the mainstream media]. What they hear and see if so far from the truth that they wouldn't believe it. Does that answer your question?

It does as ever Diana, thank you. My energies have been low this last week, and I'm wondering whether it has to do with a readjustment of living here?

Well, you have been through many changes in the last three to four years and you both say 'Oh my energies are low', but compared to other people you probably fit 10 times more things into the day than most people.[82] We give you time off don't we?

Indeed.

Perhaps we'll say no more about that.[83]

Thank you for that. I'm assuming now this closes the book? What an immense privilege. I was re-reading the book yesterday, and I can only say what a profound pleasure it is to be involved with this.

You see as people read the book, it will open their hearts for them.

Yes.

You know you may have felt it's been a long time and your frustrations about getting published, but we have to time it and the time is now. People will read this and realise there is only you, only the people on the planet that can change. And my goodness me are we proud to say it is changing, and we applaud you all that are doing this work.

Taking the planet into another dimension.

And there are more and more of you everyday, more people becoming aware. And it hasn't been easy, sometimes it has been as if you were on a never-ending road, and you are actually, because your spiritual growth is never-ending. Never give up, go forward, so your seeds of light and Love, see this planet change into the most beautiful place like it used to be without the greed; just with Love in your hearts and caring and giving. That's how things were always meant to be, but it just took a wrong turning, but now that wrong turning, that kink in the road is being straightened.

And so I leave now with all the Love and blessings here from me Diana and all the Love and blessings from your friends and family here in Spirit who tonight – there are so many of them here, so many filling your room, it really is a tight squeeze – and the angelic forces around you, lighting the way for all of you.[84]

Never, ever give up. Ever.

APPENDICES

APPENDIX A, THE CHAKRA SYSTEM AND CHAKRA MEDITATION

As already said, the chakra system is critical to your health. Rather than give a long explanation, which can readily be found in many energy healing books (especially the one the meditation is taken from–see at the end) we have put our attention on a process which balances them. By doing this, you will also become aware of the location and colours of each of the seven chakras.

With this experience, you will be directing your attention to each of the chakras in turn, first by focusing on physical sensations, then by using your imagination, your ability to create images, to create the experience of colours there. There is no difference between imagination and visualisation, except for the fact that most people believe more in their ability to imagine than their ability to visualise. They know that even children can imagine things, but visualisation... well, that's another thing.

While you will be asked to imagine certain colours in certain places, you may have impressions of other colours. If this happens, just notice what the other colours are that you are having an impression of, and then release them and replace them with a proper colour. You will be able to do this by imagining you are shining lights of the proper colour on the chakra, or painting the proper colour, or imagining something of the proper colour there. Finally you will be able to create an impression of the proper colours in the proper places, and experience the effects of that.

Now, find a comfortable position, and do the meditation as follows:

First, direct your attention to your perineum, and to the physical sensations you experience there. Feel something. Decide that what you are feeling is energy, and then decide that this energy is glowing red. If you have an impression of another colour, notice what it is, and then release it, and make it red. Have a final impression of a clear red ball of energy where you know you're red chakra to be. Hold your attention there, doing that, for some moments.

Next, move your attention or about 10 cm (4 inches), to the middle of your abdomen, and to the physical sensations you experience there. Feel something, and decide what you are feeling is energy.

Then, decide that this energy is glowing orange. If you have an impression of another colour, just notice what it is, and then release it, and make it orange. Finally, have an impression of a clear ball of orange energy where you know you're orange chakra to be, and hold your attention there, doing that for some moments.

Now, move your attention to your solar plexus. Be aware of sensations there. Feel something, and decide that what you are feeling is energy. Then, decide that this energy is glowing yellow. If you have an impression of another colour, just noticed what it is, and then change it, and make it yellow. Have a final impression of a clear yellow ball of energy glowing in your yellow chakra, and hold that experience for some moments.

Now, move your attention to the centre of your chest, where you know your green chakra to be. Be aware of sensations there, feel something and decide that what you feel is energy, and that it is glowing emerald green. If you have an impression of another colour, just notice what it is, and then release it, and make it emerald green. Hold the impression of a clear emerald green ball of energy in your green chakra for some moments, experiencing it.

Now, move your attention to the base of your throat, where you know your blue chakra to be. Be aware of sensations there, feel something and decide that what you feel is energy, and that it is glowing blue, sky blue. If you have an impression of another colour there, just notice what it is, and then change it. Decide that now, it is sky blue. Hold the final impression of a clear sky blue ball of energy in your blue chakra for some moments, experiencing it.

Next, place your attention on the centre of your forehead. Be aware of sensations there, feel something where you know you're indigo chakra to be, and decide that what you are feeling is energy. Decide that it is glowing indigo, midnight blue. If you have an impression of another colour there, notice what it is, and release it. Change it. Decide now that it is indigo, and hold for

some moments an impression of an indigo ball of energy in your indigo chakra.

Now, move your attention to the top of your head. Be aware of sensations there, where you know your violet chakra to be. Feel something, and decide what you are feeling is energy. Then, decide that this energy is glowing violet, the colour of amethyst. If you have an impression of another colour, just notice what it is, and change it. Make it violet, and hold a final impression for some moments of a violent ball of energy glowing in the violet chakra.

Finally, just relax, and notice the state of being you experience after the meditation, compared to how you felt before the experience. No doubt, you will notice how you feel better in some way, and you will therefore understand, through your experience the benefits of this meditation.

The meditation not only helps you to re-centre yourself when you need to, but also gives you an inventory of what has been happening in your consciousness just before the experience, a picture of where you are. You can expect that after the work you've done on yourself with this meditation, any out of balance conditions of been corrected, or improved to some degree.

Chakra Meditation taken from p. 164 ff., 'Anything Can Be Healed' © Martin Brofman, 2003. First published by Findhorn Press, Scotland.

APPENDIX B, BREATHING TECHNIQUES
– 20 CONNECTED BREATHS

You can do this exercise throughout the day, whenever you feel the need. However, it is recommended that for the first week you only do it once daily:

1. Take four short breaths
2. Then take one long breath
3. Pull the breaths in and out through your nose
4. Do four sets of the five breaths, that is, four sets of four short breaths followed by one long breath without stopping, for a total of 20 breaths.

Merge the inhale with the exhale so the breath is connected without any pauses. One inhale connected to one exhale equals one breath. All 20 breaths are connected in this manner so you have one series of 20 connected breaths with no pauses.

Consciously pull the inhale in a relaxed manner and let go completely on the exhale while continuing to keep the inhale and exhale the same length.

Use the short breaths to emphasise the connecting and merging of the inhale and the exile into unbroken circles.

Use the long breath to fill your lungs as completely as you comfortably can on the inhale and to let go completely on the exhale.

Breathe at a speed that feels natural for you. It is important that the breathing be free and natural and rhythmical, rather than forced or controlled. This is what enables you to breathing prana as well as air.

Since most of us have developed bad breathing habits, you might experience some physical sensations, such as lightheadedness or tingling feelings in your hands or elsewhere. If this is so, do your best to tune in and feel with detailed awareness, whilst making peace with what you are feeling. If you do this exercise daily, you will likely notice that the sensations change and become less overwhelming, and more generative of healing. This indicates that you are learning about breathing consciously and are getting direct benefits in your body.

Appendices

NOTES

1

If this interests you, please read the four *Joseph* books. 'Joseph is a highly evolved Spirit guide who is deeply worried about the fate of mankind and returns to channel important spiritual information from the higher realms through Spirit medium Michael G. Reccia.' The fourth book, 'The Fall' is a graphic account of the two previous occasions the world 'came to an end.' The books are probably the best and most comprehensive guide to the 'afterlife' you will ever read. Essential reading for the spiritual seeker.

2

Harry Edwards (1893-1976) was a printer with political ambitions (Liberal), who visited a spiritualist meeting and came across a medium who said he was an excellent instrument for spiritual healing. His first attempts were so successful and attracted such a host of visitors that he fully dedicated his life to healing. In more than 40 years of his activity, up to two thousand help-seekers per month visited him at his sanctuary in Shere, Southern England. He became famous by his public healing demonstrations. The one at Royal Albert Hall in London, attracted five thousand visitors. And we have heard about one at Belle Vue, Manchester which attracted a similar number.

As well as being a great healer, Harry Edwards was a man of true faith and humility. Amongst Harry's Spirit guides were two great scientists, Lord Lister (founder of antiseptic surgery) and Louis Pasteur (the famous French scientist).

Anne's first contact with Harry came in 1985 after a visit to a Spiritualist Church in Hyde, nr. Manchester.

3

The Healing Code are an incredibly simple but amazingly powerful process which combine prayer or intention with (Divine) healing energy through the hands (or by visualising) and using the catalyst of unconditional Love. The process was 'channelled' by American Dr Alex Loyd in 2000, after a 12 year quest to find a cure for his wife Tracy's suicidal depression; Alex would use another word to describe his experience, as his religious beliefs exclude the idea of channelling. The book, The Healing Code, which has become one of the most successful healing books every written, is co-authored by conventional and alternative doctor Ben Johnson. Ben used the Healing Code to become symptom-free from the 'incurable' Lou Gehrig's disease in 2004.

We have been running and continue to run workshops in Europe on the singular Healing Code (unconditional love, as articulated in the book-there are 24 codes in total) process since November 2010.

Visit the originator's site, www.thehealingcodes.com or our site www.thehealingcodes.co.uk for more.

4

Japanese scientist Masuru Emoto confirmed that human consciousness has an effect on the molecular structure of water after years of research. Emoto claims that positive changes to water crystals can be achieved through prayer, music, or by attaching written words to a container of water.

His water crystal experiments consist of exposing water in glasses to different words, pictures, or music, and then freezing and examining the aesthetics of the resulting crystals with microscopic photography. Very simply, the pictures to be found in his book are beautiful and highly structured when exposed to positive stimuli, and the opposite when exposed to negative thoughts, words or intentions.

This word follows a similar study by Cleve Backster, former head on the CIA's Lie Detector Division, who experimented with plants. His book, *Primary Perception: Biocommunication with plants, living foods, and human cells* (2003) showed that plants would register stronger reactions, as measured by the lie detector/polygraph, to the *intention* to harm than *actual* harm by burning a leaf for example.

5

Homeopathy is a system of medicine which involves treating the individual with highly diluted substances, given mainly in tablet form, with the aim of triggering the body's natural system of healing. It is based on the principle that you can treat 'like with like', that is, a substance which causes symptoms when taken in large doses, can be used in small amounts to treat those same symptoms. For example, drinking too much coffee can cause sleeplessness and agitation, so according to this principle, when made into a homeopathic medicine, it could be used to treat people with these symptoms. This concept is sometimes used in conventional medicine. However, one major difference with homeopathic medicines is that substances are used in ultra-high dilutions, which makes them non-toxic.

It is interesting that the person most widely accredited with the establishment and promotion of a drug-based approach in allopathic (conventional) medicine, J. D, Rockefeller rarely used drugs himself. He retained his own personal homeopathic physician until his death, aged 97.

6

Since the discovery of the Dead Sea Scrolls in 1946, the word 'Essene' has become well known. Two thousand years ago, a brotherhood of holy men and women, living together in a community, carried within themselves all of the seeds of Christianity and of future western civilization. This brotherhood, persecuted and ostracised, brought forth people who would change the world. The principal founders of what would later be called Christianity were Essenes –St. Ann, Joseph and Mary, John the Baptist, Jesus, John the Evangelist, etc.

The Essenes considered their Brotherhood/Sisterhood as the presence on Earth of the Teaching of the sons and daughters of God. The Essenes differentiated between the souls which were sleeping, drowsy, and awakened. Their task was to help, to comfort, and to relieve the sleeping souls, to try to awaken the drowsy souls, and to welcome and guide the awakened souls.

The Hebrews called them 'The School of Prophets'; and, to the Egyptians, they were 'The Healers, The Doctors'. They had property in nearly all of the big cities; and, in Jerusalem, there was even a door that bore their name: the door of the Essenes. People as a whole felt respect and esteem for the Essenes because of their honesty, their pacifism, their goodness, their discretion, and their talent as healers, devoted to the poorest as well as to the richest.

7

On May 2nd (five weeks after this was mentioned by Diana) an article appeared on Natural News web site, www.naturalnews.com, Apparently since about 2006, a US company, Ventria Bioscience has been quietly cultivating rice that has been genetically modified (GM) with genes from the human liver. With approval from the U.S. Department of Agriculture (USDA), Ventria has taken one of the most widely cultivated grain crops in the world today, and essentially turned it into a catalyst for producing new drugs.

8

Len and Janice Blood are friends of 30 years. Former political activist and engineer Len is now 'retired.' His wife Janice is a former occupational health nurse and epitomises compassion. Len is the master of (funny, at times hilarious) anecdotes about his life and people he meets. He can hold your attention for hours. Lovable Len is a man of strong opinions and the idea of alien life and reptilian bloodlines on Earth is not one he yet subscribes to...

9

Crop circles were first referred to in academic texts of the late 17th Century, and almost 200 cases had been reported prior to 1970. The designs appeared primarily as simple circles, circle with rings, and variations on the Celtic cross up into the mid-1980's in southern England. There have been over 10,000 reported and documented crop circles throughout the world, with some 90% emerging from southern England.

Because little or no scientific or factual data is provided by the media, the absence of evidence is then replaced by the ridiculing of the subject by 'experts' who dismiss crop circles as freak weather conditions or the work of people with string and planks.

Readers of this book may now know better...

10

Vasiliki Kaloutsa is a shamanic healer, based in Volos, central Greece. Since Anne and I met her in Athens in 2011, we have become close friends. Vasiliki is also a talented artist, and her husband, Fanis is a brilliant professional musician.

Vasiliki has herself had information about and from Diana, and her advice to Anne about how to present and protect this work has been invaluable.

She has helped us organise seminars in Greece and conducts Shamanic weddings in one of Greece's most beautiful regions.

11

The mainstream offer very little on this aspect. However, if you do your research you will find 'missing' chapters of the bible and the re-writing of large sections of it. Self-evidently powerful people at the time the bible was written, and institutions that followed would not want anything other than their 'spin' made available to the masses would they?

12

Anne's eyes changing colour have been witnessed by at least three people. It is not obvious to observers as Anne's eyes are closed and can exhibit REM (rapid eye movement) whilst channelling. She has also been observed by a couple of people (Clyde Hughes – www.waleshealer.co.uk, Mark W Foster – www.energiy.co.uk) 'morphing' (merging) into Diana at workshops.

13

Artemis and her twin brother Apollo were born in Delos (a small island near Mykonos in Greece) to the Greek Gods Zeus and Leto. The name Artemis means 'high source of water'. Artemis was also known as Dea Anna in Ephesus (originally a Greek city, then a Roman one; today it is in Turkey).

The name Diana means 'light'. The same goddess is Artemis to the Greeks, Diana to the Romans.

Souvenirs from Athens have on them the names Artemis or Diana, depending on your preference. The Acropolis museum in Athens is an incredible place (www.theacropolismuseum.gr)

There are many accounts of Atlantis and its most likely location. One which fits in with Diana's observations is that it was near Greece. According to ancient Egyptian temple records the Athenians [Greeks] fought an aggressive war against the rulers of Atlantis some nine thousand years earlier and won. There is also some debate as to whether this was 900 or 9000 years ago.

Another one of our very good friends is psychic artist and spiritual teacher, George (David) Fryer, www.psychicartist.co.uk. When we met George for an internet TV show in 2011, he channelled another of Anne's guides, Astonis, of… Atlantis.

Perhaps it is also interesting to reflect that two of the main themes of this book are light and water…

14

Diana has mentioned David Icke at least twice in this book, once when prompted, and later of her own volition. Like so many people who are condemned by the mainstream (for very obvious reasons), Icke's first two books, *Truth Vibrations* and *Love Heals Everything*, were spiritual books, before he moved into the arena of waking people up with his revelations. Let go of your media-conditioned view of this man. He is the towering figure in the freeing of humanity (www.davidicke.com).

15

The clothes horse! I cannot take credit for this term of mockery. My resentment of hereditary wealth and all things 'royal' blinded me to Diana's true nature. I had no time for the media creation, and believed all the negative garbage about her. However, when she began working for the mines charity shortly before her death I began to doubt my preconceptions. The image of Diana kitted out in protective 'gear' walking in minefields is etched into my memory.

16

Well Warrington Network (WWN) is a not-for-profit organisation which aims to deliver very low cost complementary therapies to disadvantaged groups or in disadvantaged areas of Warrington, a large town in the UK's north-west. Common to the therapies and healing approaches is that they help reduce stress/heal the source of illness, success and relationship issues. Anne and I are founder members. The original idea and the driving force behind this organisation is the wonderful Karen Blenkinsop, www.getmewell.co.uk. As this is written, the withdrawal of two of the original founders (ourselves, due to moving out of the area) combined with increasing pressures on Karen suggest WWN may be closing down. However we would recommend the model to others.

17

The Diana Healing Symbol is now on all our promotional material and you can buy pendants and other products to take advantage of its healing and cleansing properties. Go to the relevant section of this book or go to www.dianahealing.co to order yours.

18

We ran our 48th Healing Code workshop at Prescot, Merseyside on April 10th and although all our workshops are special, this one had quite amazing energies. No doubt this contributed heavily to our decision to run the first Diana workshop there.

19

Both books were the first containing channelled information (especially Rita Eide's) after Diana's death in August 1997. Divine Intervention, by Hazel Courtney, pub. CICO Press 1999. The Celestial Voice of Diana by Rita Eide, pub. Findhorn Press 1999.

20

Before setting off to teach the Healing Code in Greece in March 2012, Anne decided to take a book 'randomly' to read which had been recommended some months ago by another of our dear Greek friends, Dr Kalliopi Athanassopoulou. Kalliopi, a conventionally trained doctor, has used the Healing Code with many of her patients to great effect. The book in question is 'Change Your Future through Time Openings' by Lucile and Jean-Pierre Garnier-Malet, published by Kalei LLC, 2011.

One of our seminars (in Volos) was cancelled, and it gave us the opportunity to visit an intending participant, Dr Ioannis Anastasiou. Half-way through a stimulating, sometimes very intense conversation with Ioannis, he revealed he had translated an outstanding, potentially life-changing book from French into Greek. The book? 'Change Your Future…'

21

The King of Kings (1961) is an epic film directed by Nicholas Ray. It is a retelling of the story of Jesus from his birth to his crucifixion and resurrection.

22

Morphic or Morphogenetic Fields were terms brought into mainstream thinking by British biologist Rupert Sheldrake. Though purists may differ, a morphic field as referred to here is a dynamic entity which contains the consciousness or energy of humanity.

For example, when a critical mass of people are informed about anything which captures the imagination (for good or ill), it spreads to others far quicker than word of mouth or even electro-magnetic communication can explain. Terms like 'it's in the ether' have real meaning, because messages get out psychically, often without any conscious effort on the part of anyone. Clearly, we want Diana's message of Love to become part of a global 'morphic field.'

23

Anne set up her recruitment business in 1991, shortly after being unexpectedly made redundant from a major house builder.

Like all small businesses it has enjoyed growth, good times and bad times. And Anne has been very attached to it, not least because to this day, it has been a major source of income. Since her 'awakening' in 1984 after the death of her mother, she has always done some form of healing, either one-to-one sessions, teaching Reiki, or working on our NLP (Neuro-Linguistic Programming) courses.

She always expected a smooth transition from working less in the recruitment business and more as a healer.

As Diana has said, that would never be. The 'jolt' she refers to is the most recent (severe) downturn in the recruitment business and the need for Anne and myself to generate more money ourselves. So, now we both work full-time as healers, and Anne's involvement in Anne Stewart Ltd. has grown less as her daughter Karen and son-in-law Andy now run it almost completely (and very well) themselves.

24

Prescot Holistic Centre is a wonderful little place in a leafy part of Merseyside which offers a range of holistic treatments from Jan Hagar, Hilda Donaldson and Pam Smith. It is run by husband and wife John & Sylvia (www.prescotholisticcentre.co.uk).

25

Lancashire-based Healer and psychic Judith Allison had several 'insights' about Diana which she regularly shared with Anne.

26

True to form, we met Ray Crook (and his wonderful wife Diane) shortly after this, and found him to be exactly as Diana had described. This gave us both further proof, if it was needed, that the channelling wasn't in Anne's head, as both of us had had virtually no previous dealings with Ray and Diane other than by e-mail. We had no clues about his character at all.

27

Aintree, Liverpool, is the home of the Grand National, the annual horse racing event. Interestingly Anne's late father Jim was an avid horse racing enthusiast, as was Diana's former mother-in-law. I would rather watch paint dry.

28

Neale Donald Walsch is one of our greatest living spiritual teachers. An amazing man, whose books, 'Conversations with God' have been a major source of inspiration to me [Jack] (www.nealedonaldwalsch.com).

29

Julia Waterton is another one of our treasured friends. We met her 'by accident' at a talk by Phillip Day (a superb researcher into food and health, http://credence.org) a couple of years ago. Julia is a healer, therapist and feng shui expert (www.healthandwellness.me.uk).

30

As the writer of this book, I have witnessed all but three of Anne's channellings (the three written channellings in January at the beginning). On all but one occasion, Anne is calm and placid, her voice sometimes showing tiredness at the end of a long (30 minutes+) session. On this evening however, she was agitated and barely able to contain the energies coming in.

31

The magnificent Jayne Lea is the publisher of More To Life, a quarterly spiritual magazine. More To Life contains wonderful articles and features across the whole spectrum of spiritual thought and action. 'Your personal guide to spiritual enlightenment.' Jayne also has More to Life TV, which features videos with some significant people (www.moretolifemag.co.uk).

32

We live in a world full of lies and distortions from the mainstream, so who might benefit from the worldview that our DNA is fixed at birth and we are at the mercy of its 'flaws'?

Of the billions of miles of DNA inside each of us, about 95% is unaccounted for. This was prematurely or deliberately labelled 'junk DNA', with the implication that, because we didn't know what it did, it was of no use.

A detailed analysis of DNA is outside the scope of this book, except to say, that our DNA is not fixed. Anne and I have worked with a number of healings that can change it, and, as Diana says, would God create us with anything that had no value?

Similar nonsense has been talked about in relation to the Thymus and Pineal glands (i.e. they serve no purpose) in the past.

33

Maybe another stretch, or maybe not. Much has been written about weather affecting moods. We have the scientific reality that depression gets worse with low serotonin levels in winter, or in countries which have low levels of sunlight.

Diana makes the reverse case very well. And a couple of years ago, Anne was with her auntie Jean in some beautiful gardens a few miles from our home. It was raining. Anne 'commanded' it to stop. It did.

We have both stopped turbulence on planes many times. All you do is to command/have total conviction that the problem will cease, invoking God/the Creator as you do it.

34

Heart disease in all its forms is the leading cause of death in the 'developed' world. Interestingly, amongst lower income countries, it ranks fourth behind lower respiratory tract infections (pneumonia, bronchitis, tuberculosis), diarrhoea, and HIV/AIDS.

35

Diana is suggesting that it is not just what goes on here on Earth that causes misery. Apart from the influences of other planets (as in astrology), clearly she knows something yet to be revealed. My own research indicates that the Moon, Mars and especially Saturn to name but three in our own solar system may be worthy of exploration. Check out the incredible (negative) influence of Saturn on our world by reading David Icke's book, 'Remember Who You Are.'

36

Not everyone in the west recognises the existence of chakras, but for energy healers they have to be understood. If you are unfamiliar with the concept, please take to time to study it. As Diana has consistently drawn our attention to the chakras, we have included a chakra meditation process and a few more lines about them in appendix 'A.'

Our body's electromagnetic field includes the chakra system that is linked to the health of our physical form.

Chakras bring energy in to flow through our nervous systems, influencing all body tissues and functions. The major chakras which are located along the spine, parallel the major physical nerve ganglia or plexus locations. These are also linked to our endocrine system. They affect various physical systems as well as emotional and mental responses and resulting thought patterns, or habits. The lower body chakras vibrate at a slower or lower frequency than the upper centres. Each chakra has a different rate of vibration or particular tone frequency, and most writings ascribe to them particular colours. The meditation is for clearing and balancing your chakras.

37

The body has within it connecting tissue called fascia. Fascia performs a number of functions, including enveloping and isolating the muscles of the body, providing structural support and protection.

It is also has been suggested that the composition of fascia is crystalline. It is widely accepted that the body both receives and transmits information, and not just through speech. Perhaps the fascia plays a big part?

Crystals are again widely known to have many properties, not just as components in the first radios, but as healers and absorbers of harmful electromagnetic radiation.

Who says we have nothing in common with rocks and stones...

38

Fluoridation and Chemtrails are two of the biggest scams and atrocities perpetrated in the (western) world. Indeed many observers have likened them to genocide. Fluoride is the by-product of several industrial processes and we have been lied to about its role in arresting tooth decay. It does nothing of the sort and can cause fluorosis, which destroys teeth.

It was used by the Nazi's in their concentration camps in World War 2 to dumb down the inmates and make them docile. It is a poison and has been linked to cancer and kidney failure for starters.

Chemtrails are white trails left by jets in the sky. Avoid any confusion with contrails which are jet exhaust gases which evaporate in minutes.

As usual the population has been kept in ignorance of their purpose, and as we become more curious, the official reasons given for this outrage are benign weather modification. However, truth researchers have discovered that often the chemicals in these trails are heavy metal toxins which are potentially fatal over time.

Since this channelling, two significant things have come to light. Firstly, that some of the chemtrails contain aluminium nano (microscopic, invisible to the human eye) particles which are potentially more lethal than other heavy metals, and nano-particles are capable of being programmed. Check out the work of Dr Russell Blaylock (www.blaylockreport.com).

As you might expect, the second point is a cause for optimism. A very good friend of ours, truth activist Penny Pullen is a highly skilled dowser (uses dowsing rods to determine the truth of things). Penny has ascertained that the wearing of the Diana healing symbol in the form of a pendant prevents and clears problems arising from nano-particles. Contact Penny on penny.pullen@uwclub.net.

39

Yet another attack on humanity is Aspartame. This artificial sweetener is put into just about every processed food you can buy, even though sometimes its name is hidden under the label of 'flavourings.' 'Diet' and 'zero' drinks are laced with it.

Apart from it being a major health hazard (cancer, dementia, Parkinson's disease, vision impairment etc.) 'diet' drinks trick the body into believing it is getting a particular dose of sweetness, which it isn't. So, it reacts by stimulating the appetite, which causes the diet drinker to eat more...

40

Brett Lancaster is a highly skilled and all-round genuine and decent man. A senior 'Journey' practitioner (a wonderful process originated by American Brandon Bays) he runs his own unique 'Graceful Change' workshops and offers one-to-one therapy. www.gracefulchange.com

41

Deeksha, the Oneness Blessing. Chris Gibbs & Jenny Walter are two more people it is our privilege to know. Currently based in the UK's beautiful Lake District, they offer weekly sessions at their home of this gentle but powerful process. www.oneness.org.uk

42

Jay Atkinson is a ray of sunlight, a brilliant channeller and author who gives the most amazing readings about your many incarnations. She is based in North Wales and her web site is http://heartlightcottage.com

43

My personal philosophy leans towards everything being our own creation, that our reality comes 100% from within. So, I decided to test this out by asking Diana if Anne had subconsciously invited her.

The words do not do justice to Diana's reply. In the many hours of listening to the channelling, and I smile as this is written, this was a mild rebuke!

44

More Lies? This was about well-known UK author and defender of Prince Charles, Penny Junor, doing her usual thing of attacking Diana and blaming their marriage difficulties firmly at her door.

45

Dropping into the heart is part of the essence of the Diana message and forms the basis of much of the Diana Divine Healing workshops. It is very simple. We spend probably 99%+ of our time in the head.

We can move our attention around our bodies. It happens automatically if we have pain or discomfort. So, just move your point of attention to your heart as Diana suggests. Then you may ask a question of yourself. Listen for the answer from your heart; let go of your mental chatter.

Practice and you will become amazed. Your heart never lies. Your mind is conditioned by living in the material world as this book consistently points out...

46

Imagine everything you do is monitored and controlled by bureaucrats in the name of 'sustainable development' and with the goal of promoting 'the green agenda'. A global ruling body has control over all human activity, what you eat & drink, where you live, how warm or cold your home can be and how much fuel you can use is pre-determined. Dissent or rebellion is met with being sent off for 're-education'. The human population is 90 per cent lower than it is today in this futuristic society, and all remaining humans have been herded into tightly constricted cities which are run much like prisons. Does this appeal? *Welcome to Agenda 21*.

The Georgia Guidestones is a large granite monument in Elbert County, Georgia, USA. One of inscriptions reads 'Maintain humanity under 500,000,000 in perpetual balance with nature.' This monument was commissioned by 'a person or persons unknown' in 1979.

47

Jimmy is the Love of our lives. We have had the good fortune to share our homes with twelve cats since Anne and I first lived together in 1979. Every one of the previous nine was loved, and all in their own way were and are special.

Jimmy adopted us at a time of great stress in 2006 and for us he is unique.

Anyone who truly shares their lives with a companion animal, as opposed to their just occupying the same living space knows how precious the Love of and by such a creature can be.

He has had one eye removed, his other is clouded over. He is slower in movement than he was, the vet told us he was around 22 years old, but he still intrigues and inspires. And he has his own monthly column (www.thedailymews.com).

48

During the spring/summer of 2012, Greece has remained in the world spotlight, owing to the 'euro zone crisis.' The media would have you believe the problems in Greece are caused by a lazy and corrupt people, fattening themselves on money from the European Union after joining the Eurozone. They will not tell you about the state of the country after the Nazis had left it 1945, the lack of any kind of reparation, the engineered civil war that followed, the damage done by the military junta (1967-1974), the strings attached to money 'given' to Greece, the de-stabilisation of the culture through mass immigration, the conspiracy of international capital, or the plan of the 'powers that be' to terrorise a small and seemingly cowed population by 'austerity.'

We have visited Greece for over 20 years for our holidays, and for the last three years go 3-4 times/year to work over there. We are still on the lookout for a group of lazy Greeks. But then we haven't been in the parliament building or the boardroom of any bank.

And lastly, who does just about everybody on the planet, be they people or countries, owe this *debt* to? Do your research.

49

Another stream of misinformation is the unstated belief that technology can solve all our problems. However, to buy into this is to give your power away.

Self-evidently technology has brought huge benefits.

We give our power away when we expect the 'technology' of a pill to heal us. Or get in a car when it would be better to walk. Or trust the media to tell us what is really going on in the world, instead of listening to our hearts, and realising the world is just like the one depicted in the 'Matrix' film trilogy.

Taken to its limits, we sell out when we allow micro-chips to monitor our health, or worse, let those 'chipping' us take full control of our lives.

Trans-humanism, i.e. when beings are created or become half man/half machine appeals to those who have never explored their inner world, reject their own body intelligence and their true spiritual nature. Paradoxically, as previously stated, our bodies are transmitters and receivers of information.

The question remains, would you rather place your trust in Divinely sanctioned information, or that sent and gathered by the (world) 'government'?

50

Along the lines of the 'junk DNA' argument, God has created us all perfectly. The fact-driven, knowledge obsessed, linear sequential, evidence-based left brain is essential to life. Unfortunately, the 'education' system develops and encourages it at the expense of the creative, expansive and 'Divine' right brain.

51

I first became aware of short-sightedness at the age of around 12. A trip to the optician, and I have worn contact lenses and/or glasses ever since.

I have presided over and know of people who have corrected their vision problems using NLP (Neuro-Linguistic Programming).

As Diana says, 'What don't you want to see?' I have a pretty good idea what she means.

I know I can heal my sight. However, it needs to be given it a much higher priority and for me to set aside time to do it...

52

Reiki Healing is the first healing process I learned back in the 1980's. It goes back to 1922 with its originator, Japanese Buddhist Mikao Usui. It involves transmitting healing energy through the hands of the healer to the client. It works, and has thousands of practitioners world-wide.

53

Our June 2012 visit to Greece, was as always very rewarding, except this time, owing the state of the country, courtesy of the global manipulators, stressful. Austerity was really starting to bite, and many Greeks were feeling depressed or confused. And no matter how aware they are (and so many are far more awake than the UK), all have friends and family who are suffering.

Greece has huge, as yet untapped mineral and oil deposits. Wonder who would like to get their hands on that?

54

Anything Can be Healed is a brilliant book by Martin Brofman, published by Findhorn Press, 2003. Following Diana's advice, we use the chakra meditation on our workshops. See appendix 'B.'

55

During our stay in Athens, Anne revealed one night she had such a pain in her heart, she thought she was dying. Can be a bit of a trial this enlightenment stuff!

56

Manos Zavakos has been our translator on our last two visits to run healing seminars in Greece. Apart from being technically excellent, he is at one with the work we do and uses it himself.

Manos, although half my age, has much in common with me, at a personality level and circumstances of birth level. We have been working with him more closely in 2013.

57

We met Loukas Giorgiou at a presentation in Athens on June 10th 2012. I did some healing work with him and cleared a major problem he had. He talked about sharing some information on breathing and healing with us.

Diana had promised information on breathing much earlier, and we thought it may be channelled at any time. However, she also said information would get to us by people who were 'directed to us.' Had we run our June 15th workshop it would have been incomplete, because Loukas's material, given to us on June 16th, is an essential piece of the jigsaw. Please refer to Appendix 'B' and Bob Frissell below.

58

Are you ready for the debate about the origins of the human race? We have the view that God created 'mankind', it was all an accident, we started life as amoebas and eventually crawled out of the swamp, we are the product of intimate liaisons by 'aliens' and all variations in between.

Each of these perspectives has a time frame, a source of reference, and attracts both peaceful and rabid advocates.

Much of the planet and humanity's history has been kept secret, but is obviously known by the 'powers that be.' Equally, we have been subjected to a perpetual and intellectually bankrupt lie that in an *infinite* Universe, only one planet can sustain life.

The term 'alien' is used to degrade and dehumanise people from different countries so is it any surprise we are conditioned to believe extra-terrestrials-with one notable exception-are dangerous and to be resisted at all costs?

The best book on this subject I have come across is 'Slave Species of god' by South African author and visionary Michael Tellinger. Michael is wonderful man. We met him earlier this year in the UK.

59

This was the week commencing 25th June 2012. On Wednesday June 27th, one of the world's and the UK's biggest banks, Barclays, revealed it had been fined both here and in the USA for the corrupt and illegal practice of fixing and/or falsifying the rate at which banks lend each other money (LIBOR).

What has also emerged is that other major banks are being investigated for the same thing. And subsequently has been created the doctrine, 'too big to fail.' In other words, bankers can act as recklessly as they wish; the taxpayer will always be on hand.

60
In June/July 2012, the UK was experiencing some of the worst and sustained floods on record.

The good news is that the hosepipe ban levied by four water companies in the south of England has been lifted.

61
Joseph op. cit. This (cracked world) image appears in one of the Joseph work's many wonderful videos.

62
On our Healing Code workshop at Birmingham on July 14th one of our demonstrations did not go 'according to plan.' Of the 200+ we have done, all but around six have not resulted in the volunteer's two stress levels (now and in the past) going from a high of 8, 9 or 10 to 0 (completely gone) in six to ten minutes. A few have actually gone down in less than two minutes.

What is common to all these is the volunteer's difficulty in accessing and sustaining a state of unconditional love. We announce the demonstration, and then work with whoever puts their hand up first. This way we can never be accused of fixing it, but we can get some very challenging people!

The volunteer, a wonderful person who was struggling with a serious health challenge, had great difficulty in feeling

Love. One of the reasons why we get such 'miraculous' healings in these workshops is that the group joins in (without our asking) to enhance the Love energy in the room. At this workshop, the energy was so powerful, I could hardly speak.

For reasons now redundant, the volunteer became very agitated when her condition was revealed to the group. One of the first laws of healing is that you have to acknowledge the condition. However, it was obvious to everyone present that healing had taken place.

The demonstration did not follow the usual pattern and great learning ensued! The person concerned subsequently arranged for a one-to-one healing with Anne that next week.

63

Security is the double-speak watchword of our times, and one which (I should know better) presses my button. Lies, oppression, massive wasting of resources, war mongering (you get the picture) and murder all can be justified under this meaningless Orwellian word. London was turned into a militarised zone for the summer Olympics. On the morning of July 14th I had subjected Anne to a rant. You can't get away with anything!

64

A very dear friend, spiritual teacher and highly evolved human being and skilled energy 'expert', Mark W Foster had seen this. Mark couldn't lie if his life depended on it. One of the reasons we asked him to write the foreword.

65

The inspirational piece (it has become known as the Diana Prayer) from the unknown person is reproduced in 'The Beginning…' at the front of the book.

66

Nothing In This Book Is True, But It's Exactly How Things Are; You are a Spiritual Being Having a Human Experience; Something In This Book is True are Bob Frissell's books, all published by North Atlantic Press. His 20 Connected Breaths process is reproduced with permission in Appendix 'B.'

67

The 2012 London Olympics are significant in so many ways. Few people are not stirred and inspired by the achievements of the competitors. The 'powers that *(shouldn't)* be' use every opportunity to further their ambition of a totally controlled, cowed and massively diminished (in terms of numbers) human population. They, and their camp followers are obsessed with ritual and symbolism. And if you decide to use the Diana Healing Symbol, or know about Reiki you will know how the reverse (Love) energy works.

Needless to say, starting with the London 2012 logo the Olympics are awash with symbols, which contain manipulative and negative energies. Or as Diana has said, evil.

68

We had met some new people at one of our Healing Code workshops, got on with them very well and planned to run a Diana workshop at their premises. One of them had arranged to meet us here, at home, to plan how she could help promote the Diana/Spirit agenda. Everything was organised. At the last minute, she pulled out, and Anne was upset about it. With hindsight, it all worked out for the best...

69

Mind games are a well-trodden path. It is crystallized in western culture, as expressed through the media. We have the wall-to-wall doom and gloom of war, dead soldiers' funerals, murders, muggings, rapes and paedophilia. Then we have X factor, shopping, booze, 'beauty' and Cheryl Cole's hair.

However the tactic of alternately good and bad news has a little more psychological depth to it. As Diana says, it is completely designed to confuse and disorientate.

The solution? Stop watching the news, reading the lies in the papers, watching advertising and buying into the dregs of popular culture. And keep your sense of humour.

And, as John Lennon is one of the main flavours of this channelling, read the lyrics of 'Mind Games.'

70

Jan Hagar is one of the therapists mentioned previously at Prescot Holistic Centre. Diana shares our feelings for her.

71

We teach a far deeper and at first, seemingly complicated process than appears in Appendix 'B' on our workshops. Part of the process involves sending light into Mother Earth. You will find all you need from Bob Frissell's books.

72

We think Diana is referring to her nickname of 'the clothes horse', or even her saying about herself when she was alive on Earth, 'I'm as thick as a plank.' In general, we live in a world where 'intelligence' is used to rate one person against another. In truth, intelligence has many facets, more than the ability to perform well at tests.

The poor academic performance of 'royalty' is conveniently forgotten, unless it can be used as a put down, as it often was in Diana's case. If you care to investigate the idea of consciousness, and its role in elevating humanity to levels above greed and war, please check out the work of Dr David Hawkins, www.davidhawkins.org. Hawkins maintains that there is a (logarithmic) scale of consciousness, from 1 to 1000. Intellect is 'scored' at 499 (includes the likes of Einstein, Newton, Tesla etc.), whilst Love begins at 500 and rises to 599, to be followed by joy, then peace, then enlightenment. The numbers in the scale are determined through the use of muscle-testing as referred to in chapter 2. It is less complicated than it seems, but would need a chapter to explain. In simple terms? The words and essence of people like Diana, Mother Teresa, Mandela, and Gandhi will transform this world in ways impossible through intellect (and technology).

73

The Healing Revolutions is the most radical of our workshops. We cover in depth waking up to what is going on, (more) alternative healing modalities and how by changing yourself you can help change others and change the world. A bit like this book really... Go to www.healingrevolutions.co

74

Re-birthing is a tried, tested and very powerful process which acknowledges the damage birth trauma can cause, and uses a range of tools to allow the person to release the trauma and heal themselves. If this appeals to you, contact our dear friend Manos who is now a trained re-birther himself! His e-mail is e_zavakos@yahoo.gr

75

The full account of this accident may be better recorded in any autobiography. A serious car crash should have killed me, and one consequence of it (there were many), is that I was convinced life had purpose for me, though at the time I couldn't find it. The concept of a 'walk-in' is that the soul of the original 'body-holder' departs (and goes to spirit) and another soul walks in to take their place. If it happens it usually at the point where the original person is near death. The 'exchange' can be permanent or temporary. It is pre-supposed agreement is made between the two souls.

If this seems bizarre, souls usually enter the bodies of babies as we are born, so why should it seem so amazing for that to happen when a body has lost its original soul?

76

After Anne had mentioned the 'visit' of John Lennon, a couple of days later, we found ourselves (we drove down there) in Evesham, Worcestershire UK (100 miles from our then home). We walked past a room promoting a CD sale. We went in and Anne asked me to look for anything by John Lennon. There were literally thousands of CD's. After she had found nothing, and was ready to leave, I spotted a pristine, unmarked copy of a double CD of John's songs for £5.

77

Talking of Greece, we have changed our host when we go there to run seminars. We are now associated with Athens-based 'Inner Flow' run by the wonderful Effie Adamidou. For those of you who are still hanging on to the idea of coincidence, you will be fascinated to know Effie (we had never met her before) is a close follower of…the Essenes. Effie now is the principal contributor to our Diana Divine Healing Facebook page, written in English and Greek.

78

One such person is Mark McGowan, alias the Artist Taxi Driver. Mark is highly perceptive, well informed and puts his message over very forcefully. I (Jack) love his daily videos on YouTube. However, if you don't like swearing, don't watch him.

79

Gary Plunkett (gary@garyplunkett.com) is a healer, truth activist, ethical business consultant and spiritual teacher, specialising in Hawaiian healing and wisdom. A wonderful man. His de-stress seminars are brilliant.

80

A few days after this comment, Anne and I met another one of our great friends, John Campbell. We concurred that at the root of so many ills is this self-hatred. John's journey from smuggler to healer and teacher, taking in football club vice-chairmanship and becoming a fully recovered alcoholic is inspirational, and will be made into a film. John is going to spend 12 months in South Africa, using spiritual principles to raise the game of footballers in one of their top professional clubs from September onwards. It is John's dream to use the global vehicle of football to raise planetary awareness. And he will succeed. (john@miraclesrock.com).

81

The number of people required to come together to shift global consciousness varies from author to author. One puts it at 144,000. Aren't you glad it isn't seven billion?

82

I recall one 10 day spell we had a couple of years ago in Greece. We travelled to the three largest cities (Saloniki, Volos, Patras) to run seminars, as well as in Athens. The office we had to walk to frequently was positioned up a steep hill. We never stopped, sometimes working 18 hour days. The schedule would have been beyond most fit 20 year olds. All the seminars went well. You don't worry about such things when you are on a mission...

83

We moved house. In typical fashion, 2 days after we got here, we made a 250 mile round trip to run a workshop. We had planned to run two more on the next two weekends. 'Spirit' or Diana intervened. We got no takers. They didn't run. We were grateful.

84

Unlike Anne, I have no record of having *seen* those in Spirit in this world. However, as you may now know, I get a sense of them. And it was almost overwhelming at this channelling. I am truly humbled by the experience.

TOOLS AND TECHNIQUES

Here is a quick list of things Diana recommends you can do on a daily or regular basis and others whenever the need arises. If you need to revisit the origin the chapter number is given in brackets.

- **Acknowledging thoughts** [11]. Thoughts are things, treat them intelligently.

- **Angels** [4]. Ask for help.

- **Animals** [8]. Respect and care for the animal world.

- **Ask the body** [10]. Ask your body what it wants, what it prefers.

- **Beautiful thoughts** [4]. Sit with beautiful music and think of lovely thoughts.

- **Blessing** [11]. Bless what you eat and drink. Bless everything.

- **Breathing** [5; Appendix 'B']. Use breathing to relax.

- **Cellular memory clearing** [2]. Use the Healing Code.

- **Chakras** [Appendix 'A']. Open, clear and balance them.

- **Crystals** [10]. Crystals heal.

- **Discipline** [10]. Get into a daily discipline of meditation, correct breathing and drinking water.

- **Drop into the heart** [11]. As many times as you can.

- **God** [1]. Re-align with and re-connect to God.

- **Gratitude** [12]. Give gratitude to God, to others and for your life. God gives you what you are grateful for.

- **Healing. Energy Healing** [12]. Use energy healing to let go of dis-ease or whatever is holding you back.

- **Information** [2, 11, 12] Clear toxic information in the cells, welcome {loving} information from other galaxies, and be careful what you believe from the mainstream.

- **Like minds** [6]. Meet and communicate regularly with like-minded [awake] people.

- **Love**. No comment needed.

- **Meditation** [4]. Do it every day.

- **Organic food** [2]. Buy it, eat it whenever you can.

- **Prayer** [1] Pray for what you want.

- **Return unwanted thoughts** [11]. Let negative thoughts go back to their origin or God's light.

- **Sun** [3]. Have courage, face the sun, and get as much as you can.

- **Support** [1]. Help and support others; get support from them.

- **Walk in nature** [6]. 'Commune' with nature as often as you can.

ANNE STEWART

Anne, like her husband Jack was an only child. Daughter of Doris and Jim Goulden, her early years were spent in a poor area of Lymm, Cheshire, UK. She excelled at primary school, but her talents remained stifled by snobbery and discrimination by her being from the 'wrong side of the tracks.'

She had her two wonderful daughters, Karen and Janet at a relatively early age and afterwards forged a career in housing construction. Apart from becoming Sales Director with a major house builder, she won national wards for interior design.

Her (spiritual) awakening occurred after the tragic death of her mother in 1981. Whilst on holiday with Jack in Devon, a series of 'inexplicable' events culminated with the news her mother had died from a brain tumour a few days earlier on her return.

This was to open her up psychically, and soon after she decided to use her latent talents to heal rather than train as a medium. Even as recently as the early 1980's, spiritual healing was still regarded with suspicion, so Anne trained in aromatherapy, reflexology, massage and then Reiki healing (Anne is a master), which was somehow gaining acceptance.

During this time, and until very recently, she managed a small recruitment agency (Anne Stewart Associates, now Anne Stewart Ltd) which was the main source of income for the Stewart household.

As she developed her healing skills, she soon become aware that her first 'guide' was Harry Edwards (see notes). Some weeks prior to this, she had met someone in a spiritualist church in Hyde, Greater Manchester, UK who had informed her she would become a healer.

(For readers outside the UK, Hyde has a unique distinction as being 'home' to three of most reviled criminals of the last fifty years. The Moors murderers, Ian Brady and Myra Hindley, and mass murderer Dr Harold Shipman.)

Anne has a Diploma in Management, and also been trained in NLP (Neuro-Linguistic Programming), Emo-Trance, Theta Healing, Intuitive Anatomy, Reference Point Therapy, Kinesiology, Mediumship, Tarot Reading and Psychic Development.

Apart from her work as a healer and trainer, she offers 'Diana Readings' by consulting Diana to help people gain greater insights about their past, present and future.

JACK STEWART

Jack (John) Stewart was born in 1952 and was adopted as a baby and brought up by Jack and Gladys Stewart (now in spirit) in Warrington, Cheshire, UK. As a child he was encouraged to read and learn all he could. That passion for knowledge has stayed with him for life.

His restlessness and rebellious streak took him into left-wing politics in his early twenties when he also changed career from accountancy to people development. Fortunately he never took up the offer of running for parliament.

He met Anne in 1979, and they married in 1985. Anne's own progression as a healer made him realise his left-brain world of university lecturing, management consultancy and PhD's was sadly lacking (Jack has both an honours and master's degree, but gave up his PhD studies. He is also a Fellow of the Chartered Institute of Personnel and Development). He ultimately became a master trainer of NLP (Neuro-Linguistic Programming), and set up a psychotherapy practice in south Warrington in 1995. He also ran many courses in the discipline publicly and in schools.

In 2006, he met (one of his four half-siblings) Mark who had been living a few miles away, and his biological mother Winifred flew over from America to see him for the first time in 54 years. His biological father Emory may still be alive in the USA. He has plans to see his other siblings, Richard and

Kim. He met Mark's US-based brother Ray and his wife Diane at Mark's house in May 2012.

He confirmed his latent calling as a healer and spiritual teacher after discovering the Healing Code in 2010. A burning desire to help change the world from greed, war and deception to one of Love and compassion has been with him as long as his thirst for knowledge. As a hitherto staunch republican (still is!), his delight in this incredible relationship with Diana is boundless. His role in physically writing this book and ones to follow continues to delight him.

Jack's greatest Love after his wife, family (step-daughters Karen and Janet, their husbands and children) and three cats is Greece. The mere mention of the country raises his pulse rate.

Jack has co-authored three books; 1) 'The Learning Organization in the Public Services' with Janice Cook and the late Derek Staniforth, Gower 1997; 2) 'The Coaching Parent' and 3) 'The Coaching Parent Companion' with David Miskimin, Bookshaker 2005/2013. He has also co-created, with sound therapist Jeff Moran two unique relaxation and healing CDs, 'Purrfect Symphony' and 'Relax With Cats' in 2005/6. Jack intends to write his first book (by himself), 'Grin and Bear It (After All It's Only for Life)' about the power of healing and therapy to transform in 2014.

Anne and Jack follow in the footsteps of their hero Harry Edwards by teaching healing in Athens (and in other major cities). They also work with 'Spiritual Activists' when in Athens who are helping transform Greece through the power of Love with a process created by Ioannis Bouchelos called the Sound of Greece. They intend to live in Greece in the near future.

DIANA DIVINE HEALING WORKSHOPS AND DIANA ENERGY HEALING PRODUCTS

We run one day workshops all around the UK and in Europe. They have a loose framework which follows the teachings of this book.

We are finding the first ones have been populated by, as Diana has said, people who have known each other in previous lives.

However, we also know that more and more people want to experience the awakening, the opening of the heart, and final convincing that all this is as real as the book you are holding in front of you. And everyone who comes along has the opportunity to talk to and receive guidance on personal issues from Diana.

Go to our web site, www.dianahealing.co for more information, or call Anne on 01684 439397 (If this phone number no longer works, it is because we have moved yet again, so please go to our web sites for the right one).

DIANA DIVINE HEALING PENDANTS

This captures the healing energy of Diana and is a priceless gift to yourself or a loved one. It is not merely an attractive piece of jewellery. *It is intelligent and accelerates healing.* Read testimonials about it on our web site. To buy pendants go to our shop, http://DianaDivinehealing.com. Unless you receive a signed copy of authenticity from Anne it is a fake.

Our wonderful designer, Jan Holley of Lucida Glass (www.lucidaglass.co.uk) has now created 'pebbles' and a symbol is available for pets.

DIANA CARDS

54 beautiful cards containing the wisdom of Diana, as channelled by Anne. Again please go to our shop for more.

DIANA MEDITATION CD

The CD contains the Diana prayer, the 'Stardust' manifestation meditation, and the Essene meditation.